Hands-On Python and Sc

I0004156

A Practical Guide to Machine Learning

Sarful Hassan

Preface

Welcome to *Hands-On Python and Scikit-Learn: A Practical Guide to Machine Learning*. This book is designed to provide a comprehensive, hands-on learning experience in machine learning using Python and Scikit-Learn. Whether you are a beginner looking to get started or an experienced developer aiming to enhance your skills, this book serves as a practical guide to mastering Scikit-Learn for real-world applications.

Who This Book Is For

This book is intended for students, developers, data scientists, and AI enthusiasts who want to gain a deeper understanding of machine learning using Python and Scikit-Learn. Prior programming experience in Python is recommended, but not mandatory. If you are eager to explore supervised and unsupervised learning, feature engineering, and model evaluation, this book is for you.

How This Book Is Organized

The book is structured into multiple chapters, gradually increasing in complexity:

- **Chapters 1-8** introduce Python, Scikit-Learn setup, data preprocessing, and essential machine learning concepts.

- **Chapters 9-16** explore supervised learning models, including regression, decision trees, and support vector machines.

- **Chapters 17-26** cover unsupervised learning, clustering, and anomaly detection techniques.

- **Chapters 27-39** focus on hyperparameter tuning, workflow automation, and real-world applications in predictive modeling, sentiment analysis, and fraud detection.

Each chapter contains code examples and exercises to reinforce learning.

What Was Left Out

To keep the book practical and focused, some topics like in-depth mathematical derivations and complex deep learning architectures have been omitted. Instead, the book prioritizes hands-on implementation and practical applications.

Code Style (About the Code)

The code in this book follows best practices for Python and Scikit-Learn development:

- Uses **Python 3.x** syntax.

- Code is formatted for **readability and efficiency**.

- Comments and explanations are included to clarify key concepts.

- Uses commonly accepted Scikit-Learn conventions and best practices.

All code examples are tested and compatible with the latest Scikit-Learn release at the time of writing.

Release Notes

This first edition provides a structured and practical introduction to Scikit-Learn, covering a range of applications from basic data preprocessing to real-world predictive modeling.

Notes on the First Edition

This book represents a significant effort to compile practical knowledge and real-world applications for Scikit-Learn learners. Feedback is welcome for future improvements and updates.

MechatronicsLAB Online Learning

For additional learning resources and support, visit our website:

- **Website:** mechatronicslab.net
- **Email:** mechatronicslab@gmail.com

Acknowledgments for the First Edition

Special thanks to everyone who contributed to the development of this book, including reviewers, technical editors, and the Scikit-Learn community for their invaluable insights.

Copyright (MechatronicsLAB)

Disclaimer

Table of Contents

Chapter-1 Introduction to Python and Scikit-learn

Python and Scikit-learn are at the forefront of machine learning and data analysis, offering tools that empower both beginners and experts to build and deploy models efficiently. Together, they simplify the process of implementing complex algorithms and workflows.

Why Python? Python has become a dominant language in data science and machine learning for several reasons:

- **Ease of Learning**: Python's simple syntax and readability make it accessible to newcomers.
- **Rich Ecosystem**: Python boasts a wide array of libraries such as NumPy, Pandas, and Matplotlib, which complement Scikit-learn perfectly.
- **Community and Resources**: A vast community ensures abundant tutorials, forums, and documentation for problem-solving.

What is Scikit-learn? Scikit-learn is a powerful open-source library built on Python for machine learning. It is designed to interoperate seamlessly with Python's numerical and scientific computing libraries.

Key Features of Scikit-learn
- **Preprocessing Tools**: Perform data cleaning, normalization, and feature scaling with ease.
- **Supervised Learning Algorithms**: Implement algorithms like linear regression, support vector machines, decision trees, and more.
- **Unsupervised Learning**: Utilize clustering methods such as k-means and hierarchical clustering.
- **Model Evaluation**: Assess model performance using metrics like accuracy, precision, recall, and F1 score.
- **Pipelines**: Streamline workflows by chaining preprocessing and modeling steps.

Why Use Python with Scikit-learn?

1. **Seamless Integration**: Scikit-learn integrates effortlessly with libraries like NumPy, Pandas, and Matplotlib.
2. **Consistency and Simplicity**: A uniform API design ensures consistent experience across all algorithms.
3. **Extensive Documentation**: Clear and concise documentation facilitates learning and implementation.

Applications of Python and Scikit-learn

- **Predictive Modeling**: Build models to forecast sales, predict customer churn, or estimate property prices.
- **Natural Language Processing (NLP)**: Use Scikit-learn with text data for sentiment analysis or document classification.
- **Image Processing**: Combine Scikit-learn with libraries like OpenCV for tasks like object recognition and image classification.
- **Recommender Systems**: Develop recommendation engines for products, movies, or content.
- **Anomaly Detection**: Identify fraud or unusual patterns in datasets.

Python and Scikit-learn provide a robust foundation for anyone looking to harness the power of machine learning. Whether you're a beginner experimenting with your first dataset or an expert optimizing complex models, this combination offers the tools and flexibility to succeed.

Chapter-2 Installing and Setting Up Scikit-learn

Setting up Scikit-learn is straightforward, and it works seamlessly across various platforms and environments. Follow these steps to install and configure it:

Step 1: Install Python Ensure that Python is installed on your system. Download the latest version of Python from the official Python website. During installation, check the option to add Python to your system PATH.

Step 2: Install Scikit-learn Using pip

1. Open your terminal or command prompt.
2. Install Scikit-learn with the following command: `pip install scikit-learn`

3. For the latest version or pre-release, use: `pip install --upgrade scikit-learn`

Installing Scikit-learn on Different Platforms
Windows:

- Ensure pip is up to date: `python -m pip install --upgrade pip`
- Install Scikit-learn using pip: `pip install scikit-learn`

Linux:

- Open a terminal and install Scikit-learn via pip: `pip install scikit-learn`
- Alternatively, install it through your system package manager (e.g., apt for Ubuntu): `sudo apt install python3-sklearn`

macOS:

- Ensure Python and pip are installed.
- Use plp to install Scikit-learn: `pip install scikit-learn`

Anaconda:

1. Create a new environment for Scikit-learn: `conda create -n sklearn_env python=3.9`

```
conda activate sklearn_env
```

2. Install Scikit-learn via conda: `conda install -c conda-forge scikit-learn`

Raspberry Pi:
- Install Python and pip if not already installed.
- Use pip to install Scikit-learn: `pip install scikit-learn`

Step 3: Verify Installation After installation, verify that Scikit-learn is set up correctly:

```
import sklearn
print(sklearn.__version__)
```

If the version number appears, Scikit-learn is successfully installed.

Step 4: Install Supporting Libraries Scikit-learn works best with complementary libraries such as:

- **NumPy**: For numerical operations: `pip install numpy`
- **Pandas**: For handling dataframes: `pip install pandas`
- **Matplotlib** and **Seaborn**: For data visualization: `pip install matplotlib seaborn`

Step 5: Test Scikit-learn Run a simple example to ensure Scikit-learn works correctly:

```
from sklearn.datasets import load_iris
from sklearn.model_selection import train_test_split
from sklearn.ensemble import RandomForestClassifier

# Load dataset
iris = load_iris()
X_train, X_test, y_train, y_test =
train_test_split(iris.data, iris.target, test_size=0.2,
random_state=42)

# Train a model
```

```
clf = RandomForestClassifier()
clf.fit(X_train, y_train)

# Test the model
print("Accuracy:", clf.score(X_test, y_test))
```

If the script runs without errors and displays an accuracy score, your setup is complete.

With Scikit-learn installed and tested, you are now ready to dive into machine learning projects!

Applications of Scikit-learn

Scikit-learn's versatile functionality enables its use in a wide range of domains. Below are some of its most popular applications:

1. **Predictive Analytics**:
   a. Forecasting trends and outcomes in areas such as finance, retail, and real estate.
   b. Examples include predicting stock prices, customer lifetime value, or sales performance.
2. **Classification Tasks**:
   a. Categorizing data into predefined labels such as spam detection, sentiment analysis, or disease diagnosis.
3. **Clustering and Segmentation**:
   a. Grouping data into clusters for tasks like customer segmentation, image compression, or grouping similar documents.
4. **Regression Analysis**:
   a. Estimating relationships between variables, such as predicting house prices based on features like size and location.
5. **Dimensionality Reduction**:
   a. Reducing the complexity of datasets while retaining critical information for visualization or faster computation.
   b. Techniques like PCA (Principal Component Analysis) are used.
6. **Recommendation Systems**:

        a. Building systems that recommend products, movies, or other items based on user preferences and behaviors.

7. **Anomaly Detection**:
   a. Identifying unusual patterns in data, which is particularly useful for fraud detection, network security, and equipment monitoring.

8. **Natural Language Processing (NLP)**:
   a. Using text data for tasks like topic modeling, sentiment analysis, or text classification.

Scikit-learn's flexibility and ease of use make it an indispensable tool for anyone venturing into machine learning or data science.

Chapter-3 Understanding Key Concepts: Models, Estimators, and Pipelines

Scikit-learn simplifies machine learning workflows by introducing key concepts that structure the process of creating, training, and evaluating models. Understanding these concepts is essential for effective use of the library.

1. Models A model in Scikit-learn represents the mathematical relationship or pattern extracted from data. It is created during the training process by applying an algorithm to input data and learning from it. Models can be predictive or descriptive:

- **Predictive Models**: Used for tasks like classification and regression to forecast outcomes.
- **Descriptive Models**: Used for understanding data structure, such as clustering and dimensionality reduction.

Example:

```
from sklearn.linear_model import LinearRegression
# Create a linear regression model
model = LinearRegression()
```

2. Estimators An estimator in Scikit-learn is any object that can learn from data. It implements the `fit()` method to train the model and optionally the `predict()` method for making predictions. Most models in Scikit-learn, such as classifiers and regressors, are implemented as estimators.

Example:

```
from sklearn.ensemble import RandomForestClassifier

# Create an estimator (Random Forest Classifier)
estimator = RandomForestClassifier()

# Fit the model to training data
estimator.fit(X_train, y_train)
```

3. Pipelines Pipelines streamline the machine learning workflow by chaining together multiple processing steps, such as data preprocessing and model training. Pipelines ensure that all steps are executed sequentially and avoid data leakage by applying transformations only on the training data.

Example:
```
from sklearn.pipeline import Pipeline
from sklearn.preprocessing import StandardScaler
from sklearn.svm import SVC

# Define a pipeline with data preprocessing and model
pipeline = Pipeline([
    ('scaler', StandardScaler()),  # Step 1: Data scaling
    ('svm', SVC())                 # Step 2: Support Vector Machine model
])

# Fit the pipeline to training data
pipeline.fit(X_train, y_train)

# Make predictions
predictions = pipeline.predict(X_test)
```

Benefits of Using Pipelines:
- **Modularity**: Enables combining various steps like feature scaling, encoding, and modeling.
- **Reproducibility**: Ensures consistent transformations across datasets.
- **Convenience**: Reduces boilerplate code and simplifies parameter tuning with GridSearchCV.

Understanding these foundational concepts equips you to effectively design and implement machine learning workflows using Scikit-learn.

Chapter-4 Loading and Exploring Datasets with Scikit-learn

This chapter delves into loading and exploring datasets using Scikit-learn, a powerful library for machine learning in Python. Scikit-learn provides built-in datasets and tools for loading external data, enabling seamless exploration and preprocessing. Understanding datasets is a critical first step in developing effective machine learning models.

Key Characteristics of Dataset Loading in Scikit-learn:

- **Built-in Datasets:** Provides access to preloaded datasets like `iris`, `digits`, and `boston` for quick prototyping.
- **Data Loaders:** Includes functions like `load_iris` and `fetch_openml` to access structured and open datasets.
- **Customizability:** Supports loading subsets of features, target variables, or specific configurations.
- **Integration:** Datasets integrate seamlessly with Scikit-learn's preprocessing and modeling tools.
- **Exploration Tools:** Offers utilities for inspecting data structure, distribution, and summary statistics.

Basic Rules for Dataset Loading and Exploration:

- Built-in datasets are typically small and well-structured; use them for learning or prototyping.
- External datasets should be formatted as structured arrays or Pandas DataFrames.
- Ensure you understand the feature-target split and metadata provided.
- Utilize visualization libraries like Matplotlib or Seaborn for deeper insights.

Syntax Table:

SL No	Function	Syntax/Example	Description
1	Load Iris Dataset	`load_iris()`	Loads the Iris dataset.
2	Fetch Dataset from OpenML	`fetch_openml(name="dataset_name")`	Downloads a dataset from OpenML.
3	Access Features	`data.feature_names`	Accesses the feature names of the dataset.
4	Explore Target Variables	`data.target`	Accesses the target labels of the dataset.
5	Describe Dataset Structure	`data.DESCR`	Prints a description of the dataset.

Syntax Explanation:

1. Load Iris Dataset

What is Load Iris Dataset?
Loads the classic Iris dataset, which contains measurements of iris flowers across three species.

Syntax:

```
from sklearn.datasets import load_iris
data = load_iris()
```

Syntax Explanation:
- `load_iris`: A function in Scikit-learn that loads a pre-defined dataset.
- Returns a dictionary-like object containing:
  - `data`: A 2D array where rows are samples and columns are features.
  - `target`: A 1D array of numeric labels representing the flower species.
  - `feature_names`: A list of the names of the features (e.g.,

sepal length, petal width).
- o   DESCR: A description of the dataset, detailing its features and target variables.
- Ideal for understanding classification problems with a small, clean dataset.

Example:
```
from sklearn.datasets import load_iris
iris = load_iris()
print("Features:", iris.data[:5])
print("Target:", iris.target[:5])
print("Feature Names:", iris.feature_names)
```
Example Explanation:
- The first 5 feature rows (`iris.data[:5]`) display the measurements of the flowers.
- The first 5 target values (`iris.target[:5]`) indicate their corresponding species.
- Outputs feature names like `['sepal length', 'sepal width', 'petal length', 'petal width']`.

2. Fetch Dataset from OpenML

What is Fetch Dataset from OpenML?
Downloads datasets from OpenML, a repository of machine learning datasets.
Syntax:
```
from sklearn.datasets import fetch_openml
data = fetch_openml(name="mnist_784")
```
Syntax Explanation:
- `fetch_openml`: Downloads datasets by name or ID from OpenML.
  - o   name: The dataset name (e.g., `"mnist_784"` for handwritten digits).
  - o   `version`: The version of the dataset, defaulting to the latest.
- Returns a dictionary-like object containing:
  - o   `data`: A large 2D array with features (e.g., pixel values for images).

- o   target: A 1D array of labels or classes.
  - Useful for accessing large datasets not included in Scikit-learn's built-in collection.

Example:
```
from sklearn.datasets import fetch_openml
mnist = fetch_openml(name="mnist_784", version=1)
print("Data Shape:", mnist.data.shape)
print("Target Shape:", mnist.target.shape)
```
Example Explanation:
- Downloads the MNIST dataset containing 70,000 handwritten digit samples.
- The data has 70,000 rows and 784 columns (28x28 pixel images).
- The target array contains 70,000 corresponding labels.

3. Access Features

What is Access Features?
Retrieves the feature names of the dataset for reference.
Syntax:
```
data.feature_names
```
Syntax Explanation:
- data.feature_names: Lists all the column headers or feature names in the dataset.
- Helps identify the type of input data (e.g., measurements, pixel intensities).
- Essential for interpreting dataset variables.

Example:
```
print("Feature Names:", iris.feature_names)
```
Example Explanation:
- Displays feature names like ['sepal length (cm)', 'sepal width (cm)', ...] for clarity on dataset attributes.

4. Explore Target Variables

What is Explore Target Variables?

Accesses the target labels or classifications in the dataset.

Syntax:

```
data.target
```

Syntax Explanation:

- `data.target`: Contains the labels or classes for supervised learning tasks.
- These labels are integers representing categories (e.g., species or digit classes).
- Used as the dependent variable in machine learning models.

Example:

```
print("Target Values:", iris.target[:5])
```

Example Explanation:

- Shows the first few target labels for the dataset.
- For Iris, 0, 1, and 2 correspond to three species of flowers.

5. Describe Dataset Structure

What is Describe Dataset Structure?

Provides a detailed description of the dataset.

Syntax:

```
data.DESCR
```

Syntax Explanation:

- `data.DESCR`: A string description of the dataset.
  - Includes background, number of features, samples, and target labels.
  - Often specifies source and intended use.
- Helps users understand dataset context and content before modeling.

Example:

```
print(iris.DESCR)
```

Example Explanation:

- Outputs the Iris dataset description, explaining its features, classes, and use cases.
- Useful for beginners to familiarize themselves with dataset details.

Real-Life Project:

Project Name: Dataset Exploration for Machine Learning

Project Goal:

Load, explore, and summarize a dataset to prepare for machine learning.

Code for This Project:

```python
from sklearn.datasets import load_iris
import pandas as pd
def explore_dataset():
    # Load dataset
    iris = load_iris()
    # Convert to DataFrame
    df = pd.DataFrame(data=iris.data,
columns=iris.feature_names)
    df['target'] = iris.target
    # Summarize dataset
    print("Dataset Shape:", df.shape)
    print("Feature Summary:\n", df.describe())
    print("Class Distribution:\n",
df['target'].value_counts())

explore_dataset()
```

Expected Output:

Dataset Shape: (150, 5)

Feature Summary:

	sepal length (cm)	sepal width (cm)	petal length (cm)	petal width (cm)
count	150.000000	150.000000	150.000000	150.000000
mean	5.843333	3.057333	3.758000	1.199333
std	0.828066	0.435866	1.765298	0.762238
min	4.300000	2.000000	1.000000	0.100000

Chapter-5 Handling Missing Data in Scikit-learn

This chapter explains how to handle missing data using Scikit-learn. Missing data is common in real-world datasets and must be addressed before applying machine learning models. Scikit-learn provides powerful tools for imputing, transforming, and analyzing datasets with missing values.

Key Characteristics of Handling Missing Data:

- **Imputation:** Replace missing values with meaningful statistics such as mean, median, or mode.
- **Flexibility:** Supports various imputation strategies and advanced techniques like iterative imputation.
- **Integration:** Works seamlessly with Scikit-learn's pipelines and estimators.
- **Detection:** Offers tools to identify missing values efficiently.
- **Robustness:** Provides features to ensure models handle missing data during training and prediction.

Basic Rules for Handling Missing Data:

- Identify missing values using inspection or utility functions.
- Select an appropriate imputation strategy based on the dataset and problem context.
- Apply imputation consistently across training and test datasets to avoid data leakage.
- Evaluate model performance to ensure the chosen strategy is effective.

Syntax Table:

SL No	Function	Syntax/Example	Description
1	Identify Missing Data	`pd.isnull(df)`	Detects missing values in a DataFrame.
2	Simple Imputer	`SimpleImputer( strategy="mean`	Replaces missing values using a simple strategy.

		")	
3	Iterative Imputer	`IterativeImput er()`	Estimates missing values iteratively.
4	Drop Missing Values	`df.dropna()`	Removes rows or columns with missing values.
5	Transform with Pipeline	`Pipeline([...] )`	Integrates imputation with preprocessing steps.

Syntax Explanation:

1. Identify Missing Data

What is Identify Missing Data?
Detects missing values in a dataset to assess the extent and distribution of the problem.

Syntax:
```
import pandas as pd
pd.isnull(df)
```

Syntax Explanation:

- `pd.isnull(df)`: Returns a DataFrame of the same shape as df, with True indicating missing values and False indicating valid entries.
- Combine with aggregation methods like .sum() to count missing values in rows or columns.

Example:
```
import pandas as pd

data = {'A': [1, 2, None], 'B': [4, None, 6]}
df = pd.DataFrame(data)
print("Missing Values:\n", pd.isnull(df))
print("Missing Count by Column:\n",
pd.isnull(df).sum())
```

Example Explanation:

- Identifies missing values in columns A and B.
- Outputs a DataFrame indicating missing values (True) and their counts.

2. Simple Imputer

What is Simple Imputer?
Replaces missing values with a single statistic such as mean, median, or mode.

Syntax:
```
from sklearn.impute import SimpleImputer
imputer = SimpleImputer(strategy="mean")
imputed_data = imputer.fit_transform(df)
```

Syntax Explanation:
- SimpleImputer: A class in Scikit-learn for simple imputation.
- strategy: Specifies the imputation method ("mean", "median", or "most_frequent").
- fit_transform: Computes the imputation values (e.g., mean) and replaces missing values in the dataset.

Example:
```
from sklearn.impute import SimpleImputer
import numpy as np

arr = np.array([[1, 2], [np.nan, 3], [7, 6]])
imputer = SimpleImputer(strategy="mean")
filled_arr = imputer.fit_transform(arr)
print("Imputed Array:\n", filled_arr)
```

Example Explanation:
- Computes the column-wise mean: [(1+7)/2, (2+3+6)/3].
- Replaces missing values (np.nan) with the computed means.
- Outputs: [[1.   2.]
    [4.   3.]
    [7.   6.]]

3. Iterative Imputer

What is Iterative Imputer?
Fills missing values by modeling each feature as a function of others iteratively.

Syntax:
```
from sklearn.experimental import
enable_iterative_imputer
from sklearn.impute import IterativeImputer
imputer = IterativeImputer()
imputed_data = imputer.fit_transform(df)
```

Syntax Explanation:
- `IterativeImputer`: Predicts missing values using regression models.
- Works well when relationships exist between features.
- Requires enabling experimental features in Scikit-learn.

Example:
```
from sklearn.experimental import
enable_iterative_imputer
from sklearn.impute import IterativeImputer
import numpy as np

arr = np.array([[1, 2], [np.nan, 3], [7, np.nan]])
imputer = IterativeImputer()
imputed_arr = imputer.fit_transform(arr)
print("Iteratively Imputed Array:\n", imputed_arr)
```

Example Explanation:
- Iteratively predicts missing values based on the relationships between features.
- Outputs an array where missing values are estimated more accurately compared to simple imputation.

4. Drop Missing Values

What is Drop Missing Values?
Removes rows or columns containing missing data.
Syntax:
```
df.dropna(axis=0, how="any")
```

Syntax Explanation:
- axis: Specifies whether to drop rows (0) or columns (1).
- how: Determines when to drop (e.g., "any" drops if any value is missing, "all" drops only if all values are missing).

Example:
```
import pandas as pd

data = {'A': [1, 2, None], 'B': [4, None, 6]}
df = pd.DataFrame(data)
cleaned_df = df.dropna()
print("Cleaned DataFrame:\n", cleaned_df)
```

Example Explanation:
- Drops rows with any missing values.
- Outputs a DataFrame containing only complete rows.

5. Transform with Pipeline

What is Transform with Pipeline?
Combines imputation with other preprocessing steps in a single workflow.
Syntax:
```
from sklearn.pipeline import Pipeline
pipeline = Pipeline([
    ("imputer", SimpleImputer(strategy="mean")),
    ("scaler", StandardScaler())
])
transformed_data = pipeline.fit_transform(df)
```

Syntax Explanation:
- Pipeline: Chains multiple steps such as imputation and scaling.

- Ensures consistent application of preprocessing across datasets.
- Simplifies complex workflows.

Example:
```
from sklearn.pipeline import Pipeline
from sklearn.impute import SimpleImputer
from sklearn.preprocessing import StandardScaler
import numpy as np

arr = np.array([[1, 2], [np.nan, 3], [7, 6]])
pipeline = Pipeline([
    ("imputer", SimpleImputer(strategy="mean")),
    ("scaler", StandardScaler())
])
processed_arr = pipeline.fit_transform(arr)
print("Processed Array:\n", processed_arr)
```

Example Explanation:
- Performs mean imputation followed by standardization (scaling values to have mean 0 and variance 1).
- Outputs a fully processed array ready for modeling.

Real-Life Project:

Project Name: Data Cleaning for Machine Learning

Project Goal:

Impute missing values and standardize features to prepare a dataset for model training.

Code for This Project:

```
from sklearn.pipeline import Pipeline
from sklearn.impute import SimpleImputer
from sklearn.preprocessing import StandardScaler
import pandas as pd

# Example dataset
data = {'A': [1, 2, None], 'B': [4, None, 6], 'C': [7, 8, 9]}
```

```python
df = pd.DataFrame(data)

# Define pipeline
pipeline = Pipeline([
    ("imputer", SimpleImputer(strategy="mean")),
    ("scaler", StandardScaler())
])

# Process data
processed_data = pipeline.fit_transform(df)
print("Processed Data:\n", processed_data)
```

Expected Output:

```
Processed Data:
[[-1.22474487  0.          -1.22474487]
 [ 0.         -1.22474487  0.          ]
 [ 1.22474487  1.22474487  1.22474487]]
```

This project demonstrates efficient handling and preprocessing of missing data for machine learning workflows.

Chapter-6 Feature Scaling and Normalization with Scikit-learn

This chapter explores feature scaling and normalization techniques in Scikit-learn. These preprocessing steps are crucial for machine learning models that rely on distance calculations or gradient-based optimization. By transforming feature values to a consistent scale, scaling and normalization improve model performance and training stability.

Key Characteristics of Feature Scaling and Normalization:

- **Scaling:** Adjusts the range of features to a specific range, often [0, 1] or with zero mean and unit variance.
- **Normalization:** Converts data into a standard format, such as scaling rows to unit norm.
- **Compatibility:** Essential for algorithms like SVMs, KNN, and logistic regression.
- **Integration:** Easily incorporated into pipelines for streamlined preprocessing.
- **Flexibility:** Offers multiple methods tailored to different datasets and use cases.

Basic Rules for Feature Scaling and Normalization:

- Apply scaling consistently across training and testing datasets to avoid data leakage.
- Use standard scaling (z-score normalization) for features with varying units or magnitudes.
- Normalize data when focusing on row-wise transformations, such as for cosine similarity.
- Avoid scaling for tree-based models like decision trees or random forests.
- Evaluate model performance to determine the necessity of scaling.

Syntax Table:

SL No	Function	Syntax/Example	Description
1	Standard Scaling	`StandardScaler()`	Scales features to zero mean and unit variance.
2	Min-Max Scaling	`MinMaxScaler()`	Scales features to a specific range, usually [0, 1].
3	Robust Scaling	`RobustScaler()`	Scales features using median and IQR.
4	Normalization	`Normalizer()`	Normalizes feature vectors row-wise.
5	Scaling with Pipeline	`Pipeline([...])`	Integrates scaling with preprocessing steps.

Syntax Explanation:

1. Standard Scaling

What is Standard Scaling?

Transforms features to have zero mean and unit variance, commonly called z-score normalization.

Syntax:

```
from sklearn.preprocessing import StandardScaler
scaler = StandardScaler()
scaled_data = scaler.fit_transform(data)
```

Syntax Explanation:
- `StandardScaler()`: Initializes the scaler.
- `fit_transform(data)`: Computes the mean and standard deviation of each feature, then scales the data accordingly.
- Suitable for datasets with varying magnitudes or units.

Example:

```
import numpy as np
from sklearn.preprocessing import StandardScaler
arr = np.array([[1, 2], [3, 4], [5, 6]])
scaler = StandardScaler()
scaled_arr = scaler.fit_transform(arr)
print("Scaled Data:\n", scaled_arr)
```

Example Explanation:
- Computes the mean and standard deviation of each column.
- Transforms the data to have zero mean and unit variance.
- Outputs: `[[-1.22474487 -1.22474487]`
  `[ 0.          0.         ]`
  `[ 1.22474487  1.22474487]]`

2. Min-Max Scaling

What is Min-Max Scaling?
Transforms features to a specific range, typically [0, 1].
Syntax:
```
from sklearn.preprocessing import MinMaxScaler
scaler = MinMaxScaler()
scaled_data = scaler.fit_transform(data)
```

Syntax Explanation:
- `MinMaxScaler()`: Initializes the scaler.
- `fit_transform(data)`: Computes the minimum and maximum of each feature, then scales the data to the range [0, 1].
- Suitable for data where feature distributions need to be preserved.

Example:
```
arr = np.array([[1, 2], [3, 4], [5, 6]])
scaler = MinMaxScaler()
scaled_arr = scaler.fit_transform(arr)
print("Scaled Data:\n", scaled_arr)
```

Example Explanation:
- Scales the minimum value of each column to 0 and the maximum to 1.
- Outputs: `[[0.  0. ]`
  `[0.5 0.5]`
  `[1.  1. ]]`

3. Robust Scaling

What is Robust Scaling?
Scales features using the median and interquartile range (IQR), making it robust to outliers.

Syntax:
```
from sklearn.preprocessing import RobustScaler
scaler = RobustScaler()
scaled_data = scaler.fit_transform(data)
```

Syntax Explanation:
- RobustScaler(): Initializes the scaler.
- fit_transform(data): Centers and scales the data using the median and IQR.
- Useful for datasets with significant outliers.

Example:
```
arr = np.array([[1, 2], [10, 20], [100, 200]])
scaler = RobustScaler()
scaled_arr = scaler.fit_transform(arr)
print("Scaled Data:\n", scaled_arr)
```

Example Explanation:
- Scales data based on the median and IQR, reducing the influence of outliers.
- Outputs: [[-0.5 -0.5]
    [0.   0.]
    [1.   1.]]

4. Normalization

What is Normalization?

Scales each row of data to have a unit norm (e.g., L2 norm = 1).

Syntax:

```
from sklearn.preprocessing import Normalizer
scaler = Normalizer()
normalized_data = scaler.fit_transform(data)
```

Syntax Explanation:

- `Normalizer()`: Initializes the normalizer.
- `fit_transform(data)`: Normalizes each row of the dataset to unit norm.
- Useful for text classification or clustering tasks based on cosine similarity.

Example:

```
arr = np.array([[1, 2], [3, 4], [5, 6]])
scaler = Normalizer()
normalized_arr = scaler.fit_transform(arr)
print("Normalized Data:\n", normalized_arr)
```

Example Explanation:

- Computes the L2 norm of each row and scales the rows to have a norm of 1.
- Outputs: [[0.4472136   0.89442719]
      [0.6   0.8   ]
      [0.6401844   0.76822128]]

5. Scaling with Pipeline

What is Scaling with Pipeline?

Combines scaling with other preprocessing steps in a single workflow.

Syntax:

```
from sklearn.pipeline import Pipeline
pipeline = Pipeline([
    ("scaler", StandardScaler()),
    ("model", SomeModel())
])
pipeline.fit(data, labels)
```

Syntax Explanation:
- **Pipeline**: Chains multiple steps, such as scaling and model fitting, into a unified workflow.
- Ensures consistent application of preprocessing steps during training and testing.
- Reduces the risk of data leakage.

Example:
```
from sklearn.pipeline import Pipeline
from sklearn.preprocessing import StandardScaler
from sklearn.linear_model import LogisticRegression
import numpy as np

arr = np.array([[1, 2], [3, 4], [5, 6]])
labels = np.array([0, 1, 0])

pipeline = Pipeline([
    ("scaler", StandardScaler()),
    ("classifier", LogisticRegression())
])

pipeline.fit(arr, labels)
```

Example Explanation:
- Standardizes the features and trains a logistic regression model in a single pipeline.
- Ensures that scaling is applied consistently during training and inference.

Real-Life Project:
Project Name: Preprocessing Pipeline for Classification
Project Goal:
Combine feature scaling and logistic regression into a pipeline for efficient preprocessing and model training.

Code for This Project:

```python
from sklearn.pipeline import Pipeline
from sklearn.preprocessing import MinMaxScaler
from sklearn.linear_model import LogisticRegression
import numpy as np

# Example dataset
arr = np.array([[1, 2], [3, 4], [5, 6]])
labels = np.array([0, 1, 0])

# Define pipeline
pipeline = Pipeline([
    ("scaler", MinMaxScaler()),
    ("classifier", LogisticRegression())
])

# Train model
pipeline.fit(arr, labels)
```

Expected Output:

- Model trained on scaled features, ready for predictions or evaluation.
- Demonstrates seamless integration of preprocessing and modeling steps in Scikit-learn.

Chapter-7 Encoding Categorical Variables

This chapter focuses on encoding categorical variables using Scikit-learn, a crucial step in preprocessing data for machine learning models.
Categorical variables represent discrete values such as categories or labels that must be transformed into numerical formats for most machine learning algorithms to process effectively.

Key Characteristics of Encoding Categorical Variables:

- **Label Encoding:** Assigns a unique integer to each category.
- **One-Hot Encoding:** Creates binary columns for each category.
- **Flexibility:** Supports advanced methods like ordinal encoding and custom mappings.
- **Compatibility:** Works seamlessly with Scikit-learn's pipelines and estimators.
- **Preprocessing:** Ensures machine learning models can interpret categorical data accurately.

Basic Rules for Encoding Categorical Variables:

- Identify whether the categorical variable is nominal (no inherent order) or ordinal (ordered).
- Use label encoding for ordinal data when preserving order is important.
- Apply one-hot encoding for nominal data to avoid introducing spurious ordinal relationships.
- Ensure consistent encoding across training and test datasets.
- Evaluate the impact of encoding on model performance.

Syntax Table:

SL No	Function	Syntax/Example	Description
1	Label Encoding	`LabelEncoder().fit_transform(data)`	Encodes categories as integers.
2	One-Hot Encoding	`OneHotEncoder().fit_transform(data)`	Creates binary columns for each category.
3	Ordinal	`OrdinalEncoder().`	Encodes categories with

		Encoding	`fit_transform(dat a)`	ordinal relationships.
4	Encoding with Pipeline	`Pipeline([...])`		Integrates encoding with preprocessing steps.
5	Handle Missing Values	`handle_unknown="i gnore"` in OneHotEncoder		Ignores unknown categories during transformation.

Syntax Explanation:

1. Label Encoding
What is Label Encoding?
Converts categories into integers by assigning a unique number to each distinct category.
Syntax:
```
from sklearn.preprocessing import LabelEncoder
encoder = LabelEncoder()
encoded_data = encoder.fit_transform(data)
```
Syntax Explanation:
- `LabelEncoder()`: Initializes the encoder.
- `fit_transform(data)`: Learns the mapping from categories to integers and applies the transformation.
    - Accepts inputs as lists, arrays, or Pandas Series containing categorical data.
    - Maps each unique category to a distinct integer starting from 0.
- Suitable for algorithms that accept or expect numeric labels, such as tree-based methods.
- Does not increase the dimensionality of the dataset, unlike one-hot encoding.

Example:
```
from sklearn.preprocessing import LabelEncoder
data = ['cat', 'dog', 'fish', 'dog']
encoder = LabelEncoder()
encoded_data = encoder.fit_transform(data)
print("Encoded Data:", encoded_data)
```

Example Explanation:
- Assigns unique integers to categories: {'cat': 0, 'dog': 1, 'fish': 2}.
- Converts the input list into [0, 1, 2, 1].
- Useful for class labels in classification problems.

2. One-Hot Encoding

What is One-Hot Encoding?
Transforms categories into binary columns, where each column represents a unique category, and the presence of a category is marked with 1.

Syntax:
```
from sklearn.preprocessing import OneHotEncoder
encoder = OneHotEncoder(sparse=False)
encoded_data = encoder.fit_transform(data)
```

Syntax Explanation:
- OneHotEncoder(sparse=False): Initializes the encoder.
  - Setting sparse=False returns a dense NumPy array instead of a sparse matrix.
- fit_transform(data): Learns categories from the input data and creates binary columns for each.
  - Each row in the output corresponds to a sample, and each column corresponds to a category.
- Ensures no artificial ordering is introduced among categories.
- Recommended for nominal (unordered) data.

Example:
```
import numpy as np
from sklearn.preprocessing import OneHotEncoder

data = np.array([['cat'], ['dog'], ['fish'], ['dog']])
encoder = OneHotEncoder(sparse=False)
encoded_data = encoder.fit_transform(data)
print("Encoded Data:\n", encoded_data)
```

Example Explanation:
- Transforms unique categories into binary columns.
- Input `[['cat'], ['dog'], ['fish'], ['dog']]` becomes:
  ```
  [[1. 0. 0.]
   [0. 1. 0.]
   [0. 0. 1.]
   [0. 1. 0.]]
  ```
- Suitable for models like logistic regression or neural networks.

3. Ordinal Encoding

What is Ordinal Encoding?
Encodes categories as integers while preserving their inherent order.

Syntax:
```
from sklearn.preprocessing import OrdinalEncoder
encoder = OrdinalEncoder()
encoded_data = encoder.fit_transform(data)
```

Syntax Explanation:
- `OrdinalEncoder()`: Initializes the encoder.
- `fit_transform(data)`: Learns the order of categories and maps them to integers.
  - Input data must reflect an ordinal structure (e.g., `low < medium < high`).
  - Categories are automatically assigned increasing integers.
- Useful for ordinal data where the relationship between categories matters.

Example:
```
import numpy as np
from sklearn.preprocessing import OrdinalEncoder

data = np.array([['low'], ['medium'], ['high'],
['medium']])
encoder = OrdinalEncoder()
encoded_data = encoder.fit_transform(data)
print("Encoded Data:", encoded_data)
```

Example Explanation:
- Assigns increasing integers based on order: `{'low': 0, 'medium': 1, 'high': 2}`.
- Outputs: `[[0.]`
  `[1.]`
  `[2.]`
  `[1.]]`

- Ideal for ordinal variables like ratings or sizes.

4. Encoding with Pipeline

What is Encoding with Pipeline?
Combines encoding with other preprocessing steps into a single streamlined workflow.

Syntax:
```
from sklearn.pipeline import Pipeline
pipeline = Pipeline([
    ("encoder", OneHotEncoder()),
    ("scaler", StandardScaler())
])
transformed_data = pipeline.fit_transform(data)
```

Syntax Explanation:
- `Pipeline`: Chains multiple steps, such as encoding and scaling, into a single unified process.
- Reduces errors and ensures consistent preprocessing during training and testing.
- Makes complex workflows more manageable.
- Automates sequential transformations for machine learning pipelines.

Example:
```
import numpy as np
from sklearn.pipeline import Pipeline
from sklearn.preprocessing import OneHotEncoder,
StandardScaler
```

```
data = np.array([['cat'], ['dog'], ['fish'], ['dog']])
pipeline = Pipeline([
    ("encoder", OneHotEncoder(sparse=False)),
    ("scaler", StandardScaler())
])
processed_data = pipeline.fit_transform(data)
print("Processed Data:\n", processed_data)
```

Example Explanation:
- Encodes categorical variables and scales the resulting binary matrix.
- Ensures all preprocessing steps are applied uniformly.
- Outputs scaled, one-hot encoded data ready for machine learning models.

5. Handle Missing Values

What is Handle Missing Values in Encoding?
Allows encoding methods to manage missing categories gracefully.
Syntax:
```
OneHotEncoder(handle_unknown="ignore")
```
Syntax Explanation:
- handle_unknown="ignore": Ignores unknown categories during transformation, preventing errors.
  - Essential for robust workflows when test datasets contain unseen categories.
- Ensures consistent behavior across training and testing datasets.
- Particularly useful in production settings where new categories may appear.

Example:
```
import numpy as np
from sklearn.preprocessing import OneHotEncoder
data = np.array([['cat'], ['dog'], ['fish'], [None]])
encoder = OneHotEncoder(sparse=False,
handle_unknown="ignore")
encoded_data = encoder.fit_transform(data)
print("Encoded Data:\n", encoded_data)
```

Example Explanation:

- Handles missing or unexpected values (None) by ignoring them during encoding.
- Outputs: [[1. 0. 0.]
  [0. 1. 0.]
  [0. 0. 1.]
  [0. 0. 0.]]
- Ensures the workflow remains error-free, even with incomplete data.

Real-Life Project:

Project Name: Categorical Data Preprocessing Pipeline

Project Goal:

Create a pipeline to encode categorical features and preprocess data for machine learning.

Code for This Project:

```python
import numpy as np
from sklearn.pipeline import Pipeline
from sklearn.compose import ColumnTransformer
from sklearn.preprocessing import OneHotEncoder,
StandardScaler

# Example dataset
data = np.array([
    ['low', 10],
    ['medium', 20],
    ['high', 30],
    ['medium', 40]
])

categorical_features = [0]
numerical_features = [1]

preprocessor = ColumnTransformer(
    transformers=[
        ("cat", OneHotEncoder(), categorical_features),
```

```python
        ("num", StandardScaler(), numerical_features)
    ]
)

pipeline = Pipeline([
    ("preprocessor", preprocessor)
])

processed_data = pipeline.fit_transform(data)
print("Processed Data:\n", processed_data)
```

Expected Output:

- Encodes categorical variables using one-hot encoding and scales numeric features.
- Outputs a preprocessed dataset ready for machine learning.

Chapter-8 Feature Selection and Dimensionality Reduction

This chapter explores feature selection and dimensionality reduction techniques in Scikit-learn, essential steps for optimizing machine learning models. Feature selection identifies the most relevant features in a dataset, while dimensionality reduction transforms features into a lower-dimensional space. These techniques help improve model performance, reduce overfitting, and enhance interpretability.

Key Characteristics of Feature Selection and Dimensionality Reduction:

- **Feature Selection:** Selects the most important features based on statistical methods or model performance.
- **Dimensionality Reduction:** Combines or projects features into fewer dimensions while retaining essential information.
- **Improves Efficiency:** Reduces computation time and memory usage.
- **Enhances Model Performance:** Mitigates the risk of overfitting by eliminating irrelevant or redundant features.
- **Compatibility:** Seamlessly integrates with Scikit-learn pipelines and workflows.

Basic Rules for Feature Selection and Dimensionality Reduction:

- Use feature selection methods for interpretable datasets or to identify key predictors.
- Apply dimensionality reduction for high-dimensional data to improve computational efficiency.
- Combine these techniques with cross-validation to ensure robustness.
- Ensure that selected or reduced features are consistent across training and test datasets.

Syntax Table:

SL No	Function	Syntax/Example	Description
1	Univariate Feature Selection	`SelectKBest(score_func, k)`	Selects top k features based on statistical tests.
2	Recursive Feature Elimination	`RFE(estimator, n_features_to_select)`	Iteratively selects features by ranking.
3	Principal Component Analysis (PCA)	`PCA(n_components)`	Reduces dimensions using linear projections.
4	Variance Threshold	`VarianceThreshold(threshold)`	Removes features with low variance.
5	Pipeline Integration	`Pipeline([...])`	Combines selection/reduction with preprocessing steps.

Syntax Explanation:

1. Univariate Feature Selection

What is Univariate Feature Selection?

Selects the most relevant features based on statistical tests, such as ANOVA or chi-square tests.

Syntax:

```
from sklearn.feature_selection import SelectKBest,
f_classif
selector = SelectKBest(score_func=f_classif, k=5)
selected_features = selector.fit_transform(X, y)
```

Syntax Explanation:

- `SelectKBest`: Initializes the feature selector.
- `score_func`: Specifies the statistical test to evaluate features.
  - `f_classif`: ANOVA F-value for classification tasks.
  - `chi2`: Chi-square test for non-negative features.

- k: Number of top features to select.
- `fit_transform(X, y)`: Fits the selector on X (features) and y (target) and returns the selected features.

Example:
```
from sklearn.feature_selection import SelectKBest,
f_classif
import numpy as np


X = np.random.rand(100, 10)   # 100 samples, 10 features
y = np.random.randint(0, 2, size=100)   # Binary target
selector = SelectKBest(score_func=f_classif, k=3)
X_selected = selector.fit_transform(X, y)
print("Selected Features Shape:", X_selected.shape)
```
Example Explanation:
- Selects the top 3 features most correlated with the target variable.
- Outputs the reduced dataset with 3 columns (selected features).

2. Recursive Feature Elimination (RFE)

What is Recursive Feature Elimination?
Recursively removes the least important features using an estimator to determine feature importance.

Syntax:
```
from sklearn.feature_selection import RFE
from sklearn.ensemble import RandomForestClassifier
selector = RFE(estimator=RandomForestClassifier(),
n_features_to_select=5)
X_selected = selector.fit_transform(X, y)
```
Syntax Explanation:
- RFE: Initializes the recursive feature eliminator.
- `estimator`: The model used to rank feature importance (e.g., RandomForestClassifier).
- `n_features_to_select`: Specifies the number of features to keep.
- `fit_transform(X, y)`: Fits the estimator to X and y and removes less important features iteratively.

Example:
```
from sklearn.feature_selection import RFE
from sklearn.linear_model import LogisticRegression
import numpy as np

X = np.random.rand(50, 8)  # 50 samples, 8 features
y = np.random.randint(0, 2, size=50)
selector = RFE(estimator=LogisticRegression(),
n_features_to_select=3)
X_selected = selector.fit_transform(X, y)
print("Selected Features Shape:", X_selected.shape)
```
Example Explanation:
- Uses logistic regression to rank feature importance.
- Selects the top 3 features iteratively.
- Outputs a reduced dataset with 3 features.

3. Principal Component Analysis (PCA)

What is PCA?
Reduces the dimensionality of data by projecting it onto a smaller number of components while retaining most of the variance.
Syntax:
```
from sklearn.decomposition import PCA
pca = PCA(n_components=2)
X_reduced = pca.fit_transform(X)
```

Syntax Explanation:
- PCA: Initializes the dimensionality reduction technique.
- n_components: Specifies the number of principal components to keep.
- fit_transform(X): Computes the principal components and reduces the dataset to the specified dimensions.
- Suitable for high-dimensional datasets where features are correlated.

Example:

```
from sklearn.decomposition import PCA
import numpy as np

X = np.random.rand(100, 20)   # 100 samples, 20 features
pca = PCA(n_components=5)
X_reduced = pca.fit_transform(X)
print("Reduced Features Shape:", X_reduced.shape)
```

Example Explanation:

- Reduces the dataset from 20 features to 5 principal components.
- Retains most of the variance in the dataset.

4. Variance Threshold

What is Variance Threshold?
Removes features with variance below a specified threshold.

Syntax:

```
from sklearn.feature_selection import VarianceThreshold
selector = VarianceThreshold(threshold=0.01)
X_selected = selector.fit_transform(X)
```

Syntax Explanation:

- VarianceThreshold: Removes features with low variability.
- threshold: Minimum variance required for a feature to be retained.
- Suitable for filtering out constant or near-constant features.

Example:

```
import numpy as np
from sklearn.feature_selection import VarianceThreshold

X = np.array([[1, 0, 0], [0, 0, 0], [1, 0, 0]])
selector = VarianceThreshold(threshold=0.1)
X_selected = selector.fit_transform(X)
print("Selected Features Shape:", X_selected.shape)
```

Example Explanation:

- Removes columns with variance less than 0.1.
- Outputs a dataset with features meeting the variance threshold.

5. Pipeline Integration

What is Pipeline Integration?
Combines feature selection or dimensionality reduction with other preprocessing steps into a unified workflow.

Syntax:

```
from sklearn.pipeline import Pipeline
pipeline = Pipeline([
    ("pca", PCA(n_components=5)),
    ("classifier", LogisticRegression())
])
pipeline.fit(X, y)
```

Syntax Explanation:

- Pipeline: Chains multiple steps, such as PCA and model fitting, into a single process.
- Automates feature reduction and ensures consistency across datasets.
- Simplifies complex machine learning workflows.

Example:

```
from sklearn.pipeline import Pipeline
from sklearn.decomposition import PCA
from sklearn.ensemble import RandomForestClassifier
import numpy as np

X = np.random.rand(150, 50)
y = np.random.randint(0, 2, size=150)

pipeline = Pipeline([
    ("pca", PCA(n_components=10)),
    ("classifier", RandomForestClassifier())
])
pipeline.fit(X, y)
```

Example Explanation:

- Reduces the dataset to 10 components using PCA.
- Trains a random forest classifier on the reduced dataset.
- Ensures preprocessing and modeling steps are applied consistently.

Real-Life Project:

Project Name: Feature Optimization Pipeline

Project Goal:

Create a preprocessing pipeline to select or reduce features and train a model efficiently.

Code for This Project:

```python
from sklearn.pipeline import Pipeline
from sklearn.feature_selection import SelectKBest,
f_classif
from sklearn.ensemble import GradientBoostingClassifier
import numpy as np

# Example dataset
X = np.random.rand(200, 20)
y = np.random.randint(0, 2, size=200)

pipeline = Pipeline([
    ("feature_selection",
SelectKBest(score_func=f_classif, k=10)),
    ("classifier", GradientBoostingClassifier())
])

pipeline.fit(X, y)
```

Expected Output:

- Selects the 10 most relevant features and trains a gradient boosting classifier.
- Demonstrates efficient feature selection and modeling in a single workflow.

Chapter-9 Splitting Data for Training and Testing

This chapter explores techniques for splitting datasets into training and testing subsets using Scikit-learn. Splitting data ensures fair evaluation of machine learning models by testing them on unseen data, reducing the risk of overfitting and providing a realistic assessment of performance.

Key Characteristics of Data Splitting:

- **Training Set:** Used to train the model.
- **Testing Set:** Used to evaluate the model's performance on unseen data.
- **Stratification:** Maintains the distribution of target classes in training and testing subsets.
- **Randomization:** Shuffles data to prevent order bias during splitting.
- **Reproducibility:** Ensures consistency across runs by setting random seeds.

Basic Rules for Splitting Data:

- Use an appropriate ratio for training and testing sets, typically 70-30 or 80-20.
- Stratify the split for imbalanced datasets to maintain class distributions.
- Avoid data leakage by splitting before preprocessing steps like scaling or encoding.
- Use cross-validation for robust evaluation, especially with smaller datasets.

Syntax Table:

SL No	Function	Syntax/Example	Description
1	Basic Train-Test Split	`train_test_split( X, y)`	Splits data into training and testing subsets.
2	Stratified Split	`train_test_split( X, y, stratify=y)`	Ensures class distribution is

				preserved.
3	Control Random State	`train_test_split( X, y, random_state=42)`	Ensures reproducible results.
4	Split with Custom Ratios	`train_test_split( X, y, test_size=0.2)`	Specifies the size of the test set.
5	Split for Validation Set	Split training data further for validation.	Enables hyperparameter tuning.

Syntax Explanation:

1. Basic Train-Test Split
What is Train-Test Split?
Splits a dataset into training and testing subsets for model training and evaluation.
Syntax:
```
from sklearn.model_selection import train_test_split
X_train, X_test, y_train, y_test = train_test_split(X,
y)
```
Syntax Explanation:
- `train_test_split`: Function to split features (X) and labels (y) into training and testing sets.
- Returns four subsets:
  - `X_train, y_train`: Training features and labels.
  - `X_test, y_test`: Testing features and labels.
- The default split ratio is 75% training and 25% testing.
- Use this function to evaluate the model on unseen data.

Example:
```
from sklearn.model_selection import train_test_split
import numpy as np
X = np.random.rand(100, 5)  # 100 samples, 5 features
y = np.random.randint(0, 2, 100)  # Binary target
X_train, X_test, y_train, y_test = train_test_split(X,
y)
print("Training Set Shape:", X_train.shape)
```

```
print("Testing Set Shape:", X_test.shape)
```

Example Explanation:
- Splits the dataset into 75 samples for training and 25 for testing.
- Ensures the model is evaluated on data it hasn't seen during training.

2. Stratified Split

What is Stratified Split?
Ensures that the class distribution in the training and testing sets matches the original dataset.
Syntax:
```
train_test_split(X, y, stratify=y)
```

Syntax Explanation:
- `stratify=y`: Ensures proportional representation of classes in both subsets.
- Particularly useful for imbalanced datasets where some classes are underrepresented.

Example:
```
from sklearn.model_selection import train_test_split
import numpy as np

X = np.random.rand(100, 5)
y = np.concatenate([np.zeros(80), np.ones(20)])  #
Imbalanced target
X_train, X_test, y_train, y_test = train_test_split(X,
y, stratify=y)
print("Class Distribution in Train Set:",
np.bincount(y_train.astype(int)))
print("Class Distribution in Test Set:",
np.bincount(y_test.astype(int)))
```

Example Explanation:
- Splits the dataset while preserving the class proportions of 80% zeros and 20% ones.

- Outputs the same proportions in both training and testing sets.

3. Control Random State

What is Control Random State?
Ensures consistent data splits across multiple runs by setting a fixed random seed.
Syntax:
```
train_test_split(X, y, random_state=42)
```

Syntax Explanation:
- `random_state`: An integer seed for random number generation.
- Guarantees the same split every time the code is run.
- Useful for reproducibility in experiments.

Example:
```
from sklearn.model_selection import train_test_split
import numpy as np

X = np.random.rand(100, 5)
y = np.random.randint(0, 2, 100)
X_train1, X_test1, y_train1, y_test1 =
train_test_split(X, y, random_state=42)
X_train2, X_test2, y_train2, y_test2 =
train_test_split(X, y, random_state=42)
print("Is Split Identical:", np.array_equal(X_train1,
X_train2))
```

Example Explanation:
- Ensures identical splits (True) across both runs due to the same random seed.

4. Split with Custom Ratios

What is Split with Custom Ratios?
Allows specifying the proportion of the dataset to allocate to the test set.
Syntax:
```
train_test_split(X, y, test_size=0.2)
```

Syntax Explanation:

- `test_size`: Fraction of the dataset to use for testing (e.g., 0.2 for 20%).
- Controls the balance between training and testing data.
- Accepts float values (fraction) or integer values (number of samples).

Example:

```
from sklearn.model_selection import train_test_split
import numpy as np
X = np.random.rand(100, 5)
y = np.random.randint(0, 2, 100)
X_train, X_test, y_train, y_test = train_test_split(X, y, test_size=0.2)
print("Training Set Size:", len(X_train))
print("Testing Set Size:", len(X_test))
```

Example Explanation:

- Allocates 80% (80 samples) for training and 20% (20 samples) for testing.

5. Split for Validation Set

What is Split for Validation Set?

Divides the training set further to create a validation set for hyperparameter tuning.

Syntax:

```
X_train, X_val, y_train, y_val = train_test_split(X_train, y_train, test_size=0.2)
```

Syntax Explanation:

- Creates a validation set by splitting the training set further.
- Ensures the test set remains untouched during hyperparameter optimization.
- Useful for selecting model parameters without biasing test set results.

Example:

```
from sklearn.model_selection import train_test_split
import numpy as np

X = np.random.rand(100, 5)
y = np.random.randint(0, 2, 100)
X_train, X_test, y_train, y_test = train_test_split(X,
y, test_size=0.2, random_state=42)
X_train, X_val, y_train, y_val =
train_test_split(X_train, y_train, test_size=0.25,
random_state=42)
print("Training Set Size:", len(X_train))
print("Validation Set Size:", len(X_val))
print("Testing Set Size:", len(X_test))
```

Example Explanation:
- Splits the dataset into 60% training, 20% validation, and 20% testing.
- Ensures a separate validation set for unbiased hyperparameter tuning.

Real-Life Project:

Project Name: Data Splitting for Model Evaluation

Project Goal:

Split data into training, validation, and testing sets for robust evaluation of a machine learning model.

Code for This Project:

```
from sklearn.model_selection import train_test_split
import numpy as np

# Generate example dataset
X = np.random.rand(1000, 10)
y = np.random.randint(0, 2, 1000)

# Split into training and testing sets
X_train, X_test, y_train, y_test = train_test_split(X,
```

```
y, test_size=0.2, random_state=42)

# Further split the training set into training and
validation sets
X_train, X_val, y_train, y_val =
train_test_split(X_train, y_train, test_size=0.25,
random_state=42)

print("Training Set Shape:", X_train.shape)
print("Validation Set Shape:", X_val.shape)
print("Testing Set Shape:", X_test.shape)
```

Expected Output:

- Training set: 60% of the dataset.
- Validation set: 20% of the dataset.
- Testing set: 20% of the dataset.
- Ensures fair model evaluation and hyperparameter tuning.

Introduction to Supervised Learning with Scikit-learn

This chapter introduces supervised learning, a foundational approach in machine learning, using Scikit-learn. Supervised learning involves training models on labeled data to predict outputs for unseen inputs. Scikit-learn provides a wide array of tools to implement and evaluate supervised learning models effectively.

Key Characteristics of Supervised Learning:

- **Labeled Data:** Requires input data (X) and corresponding labels (y).
- **Predictive Modeling:** Learns a mapping between inputs and outputs to make predictions.
- **Two Main Types:**
  - **Classification:** Predicts discrete labels (e.g., spam vs. non-spam).
  - **Regression:** Predicts continuous values (e.g., house prices).
- **Model Evaluation:** Assesses model performance using metrics such as accuracy, precision, and mean squared error.
- **Integration:** Easily implemented with Scikit-learn's intuitive interface and prebuilt algorithms.

Basic Rules for Supervised Learning:

- Start with data preprocessing, such as handling missing values and encoding categorical variables.
- Split data into training, validation, and testing sets to ensure fair evaluation.
- Choose a model appropriate for the problem type (classification or regression).
- Use cross-validation for robust performance evaluation.
- Fine-tune hyperparameters to optimize model performance.

Syntax Table:

SL No	Function	Syntax/Example	Description
1	Classification Model	`LogisticRegres sion()`	Implements a logistic regression classifier.
2	Regression Model	`LinearRegressi on()`	Implements a linear regression model.
3	Fit Model	`model.fit(X_tr ain, y_train)`	Trains the model on the training data.
4	Predict Outcomes	`model.predict( X_test)`	Makes predictions on new data.
5	Evaluate Model	`accuracy_score (y_test, y_pred)`	Calculates the model's performance.

Syntax Explanation:

1. Classification Model

What is a Classification Model?
A classification model predicts discrete class labels based on input features.

Syntax:
```
from sklearn.linear_model import LogisticRegression
classifier = LogisticRegression()
```

Syntax Explanation:
- `LogisticRegression()`: Initializes a logistic regression classifier.
- Suitable for binary or multi-class classification tasks.
- Provides options for regularization (e.g., L1, L2) to prevent overfitting.

Example:

```
from sklearn.linear_model import LogisticRegression
import numpy as np

X_train = np.random.rand(100, 5)
y_train = np.random.randint(0, 2, 100)
classifier = LogisticRegression()
classifier.fit(X_train, y_train)
```

Example Explanation:

- Trains a logistic regression model on randomly generated training data.
- Prepares the model for making predictions on unseen data.

2. Regression Model

What is a Regression Model?

A regression model predicts continuous values based on input features.

Syntax:

```
from sklearn.linear_model import LinearRegression
regressor = LinearRegression()
```

Syntax Explanation:

- LinearRegression(): Initializes a linear regression model.
- Finds the best-fit line that minimizes the mean squared error between predictions and actual values.
- Ideal for continuous target variables.

Example:

```
from sklearn.linear_model import LinearRegression
import numpy as np
X_train = np.random.rand(100, 3)
y_train = np.random.rand(100)
regressor = LinearRegression()
regressor.fit(X_train, y_train)
```

Example Explanation:

- Trains a linear regression model on randomly generated training data.
- Learns the relationship between input features and the target variable.

3. Fit Model

What is Fitting a Model?
Fitting a model involves training it on the provided data.
Syntax:
```
model.fit(X_train, y_train)
```

Syntax Explanation:
- fit(X_train, y_train): Uses the training data (X_train) and labels (y_train) to train the model.
- Updates the model's parameters to minimize the error.

Example:
```
from sklearn.tree import DecisionTreeClassifier
import numpy as np


X_train = np.random.rand(80, 4)
y_train = np.random.randint(0, 2, 80)
classifier = DecisionTreeClassifier()
classifier.fit(X_train, y_train)
```
Example Explanation:
- Fits a decision tree classifier to the training data.
- Prepares the model for predicting class labels on unseen data.

4. Predict Outcomes

What is Predicting Outcomes?
Predicts outputs (labels or values) for new data using the trained model.
Syntax:
```
y_pred = model.predict(X_test)
```

Syntax Explanation:
- predict(X_test): Generates predictions for the input features in X_test.
- Returns predicted labels (classification) or values (regression).

Example:
```
from sklearn.linear_model import LogisticRegression
import numpy as np
```

```
X_test = np.random.rand(20, 5)
classifier = LogisticRegression()
y_pred = classifier.predict(X_test)
```

Example Explanation:
- Generates predictions for the test dataset using the trained logistic regression model.

5. Evaluate Model

What is Model Evaluation?

Assesses the performance of the trained model using appropriate metrics.

Syntax:
```
from sklearn.metrics import accuracy_score
evaluation = accuracy_score(y_test, y_pred)
```

Syntax Explanation:
- accuracy_score: Calculates the proportion of correct predictions in classification tasks.
- Other metrics include precision, recall, F1-score (classification), and mean squared error (regression).

Example:
```
from sklearn.metrics import accuracy_score
import numpy as np

y_test = np.array([0, 1, 1, 0])
y_pred = np.array([0, 1, 0, 0])
evaluation = accuracy_score(y_test, y_pred)
print("Accuracy:", evaluation)
```

Example Explanation:
- Compares the predicted labels (y_pred) with the true labels (y_test).
- Outputs the accuracy of the model.

Real-Life Project:
Project Name: Building a Classification Model
Project Goal:

Train a supervised learning model to classify data and evaluate its performance.

Code for This Project:

```python
from sklearn.datasets import load_iris
from sklearn.model_selection import train_test_split
from sklearn.linear_model import LogisticRegression
from sklearn.metrics import accuracy_score

# Load dataset
iris = load_iris()
X, y = iris.data, iris.target

# Split data into training and testing sets
X_train, X_test, y_train, y_test = train_test_split(X,
y, test_size=0.2, random_state=42)

# Train logistic regression model
classifier = LogisticRegression(max_iter=200)
classifier.fit(X_train, y_train)

# Make predictions
y_pred = classifier.predict(X_test)

# Evaluate the model
accuracy = accuracy_score(y_test, y_pred)
print("Accuracy:", accuracy)
```

Expected Output:
- Outputs the accuracy of the logistic regression model on the Iris dataset.
- Demonstrates the workflow for training, predicting, and evaluating a supervised learning model.

Chapter-10 Linear Regression with Scikit-learn

This chapter explores linear regression, a fundamental algorithm in supervised learning, implemented using Scikit-learn. Linear regression models the relationship between input features and a continuous target variable by fitting a linear equation to the data.

Key Characteristics of Linear Regression:

- **Simple and Interpretable:** Easy to understand and interpret results.
- **Continuous Target Variable:** Predicts numeric outcomes (e.g., house prices).
- **Linearity Assumption:** Assumes a linear relationship between features and the target variable.
- **Optimization:** Uses Ordinary Least Squares (OLS) to minimize the error.
- **Scalability:** Efficient for small to medium-sized datasets.

Basic Rules for Linear Regression:

- Ensure the relationship between features and the target is approximately linear.
- Remove or address multicollinearity among features to improve model stability.
- Normalize or scale features if they differ in magnitude.
- Split data into training and testing subsets to evaluate model performance.

Syntax Table:

SL No	Function	Syntax/Example	Description
1	Initialize Model	`LinearRegression()`	Creates a linear regression model instance.
2	Train Model	`model.fit(X_train, y_train)`	Fits the model to the training data.
3	Predict Outcomes	`model.predict(X_test)`	Generates predictions for input features.
4	Evaluate	`mean_squared_erro`	Calculates the error of

		Model	r(y_test, y_pred)	predictions.
5		Get Coefficien ts	model.coef_	Retrieves the coefficients of the model.

Syntax Explanation:

1. Initialize Model

What is Initializing a Linear Regression Model?
Creates an instance of the linear regression model.
Syntax:
```
from sklearn.linear_model import LinearRegression
model = LinearRegression()
```
Syntax Explanation:
- `LinearRegression()`: Initializes the model with default settings.
    - `fit_intercept`: By default set to `True`, it calculates the intercept of the line. If set to `False`, the line passes through the origin.
    - `normalize`: Deprecated since Scikit-learn 0.24. Use `StandardScaler` instead for normalization.
- Prepares the model for training and prediction.
- Ensures the framework for finding the best-fit line in the next steps.

Example:
```
from sklearn.linear_model import LinearRegression
model = LinearRegression()
```

Example Explanation:
- Creates a linear regression model ready to be trained on data.

2. Train Model

What is Training a Linear Regression Model?
Fits the model to the training data by finding the best-fit line.
Syntax:

```
model.fit(X_train, y_train)
```

Syntax Explanation:

- `fit(X_train, y_train)`: Uses the training features (`X_train`) and corresponding target values (`y_train`) to compute the parameters of the linear model.
  - The model determines the slope (coefficients) and intercept that minimize the residual sum of squares between the predicted and actual values.
  - The input `X_train` must be a 2D array, while `y_train` can be a 1D array.
- After fitting, the model is ready to make predictions.

Example:
```
from sklearn.linear_model import LinearRegression
import numpy as np

X_train = np.array([[1], [2], [3], [4]])
y_train = np.array([2.5, 3.5, 4.5, 5.5])
model = LinearRegression()
model.fit(X_train, y_train)
```
Example Explanation:

- Trains the model on a simple dataset where `X_train` represents features and `y_train` represents targets.
- Learns the relationship: `y = 1 + x`.
- The intercept is `1.0`, and the coefficient for x is also `1.0`.

3. Predict Outcomes

What is Predicting Outcomes?
Generates predictions for new data using the trained model.
Syntax:
```
y_pred = model.predict(X_test)
```
Syntax Explanation:

- `predict(X_test)`: Computes predicted values for the test features (`X_test`) using the learned coefficients and intercept.
  - The formula is `y_pred = intercept + coefficient * X_test`.

o   Input X_test must be in the same format as X_train during fitting.
- Returns an array of predictions corresponding to the input samples.

Example:
```
X_test = np.array([[5], [6]])
y_pred = model.predict(X_test)
print("Predictions:", y_pred)
```

Example Explanation:
- Predicts target values for X_test based on the learned relationship.
- Outputs predictions like [6.5, 7.5], reflecting the equation y = 1 + x.

4. Evaluate Model

What is Model Evaluation?
Assesses the model's performance by comparing predictions with actual values.

Syntax:
```
from sklearn.metrics import mean_squared_error
error = mean_squared_error(y_test, y_pred)
```

Syntax Explanation:
- mean_squared_error(y_test, y_pred): Measures the average squared differences between actual values (y_test) and predictions (y_pred).
  o   Indicates how close predictions are to the true target values.
  o   A lower value represents better model performance.
- Suitable for regression tasks as it penalizes larger errors more heavily.

Example:
```
from sklearn.metrics import mean_squared_error
y_test = np.array([6.5, 7.5])
y_pred = np.array([6.4, 7.6])
error = mean_squared_error(y_test, y_pred)
```

```
print("Mean Squared Error:", error)
```
Example Explanation:
- Compares predictions with true values and calculates the error.
- Outputs an error value of 0.01, indicating the model performed well.

5. Get Coefficients

What are Model Coefficients?
Represent the weights assigned to each feature in the linear equation.
Syntax:
```
coefficients = model.coef_
```
Syntax Explanation:
- coef_: A NumPy array containing the coefficients (slopes) of the features.
  - Each value represents the change in the target variable for a one-unit increase in the corresponding feature, assuming other features remain constant.
- Does not include the intercept term; use model.intercept_ for that.

Example:
```
coefficients = model.coef_
print("Coefficients:", coefficients)
```
Example Explanation:
- Outputs the weights of the features, such as [1.0], indicating a direct linear relationship.
- If there are multiple features, coef_ will contain one coefficient per feature.

Real-Life Project:
Project Name: Predicting House Prices
Project Goal:
Build a linear regression model to predict house prices based on features like size, location, and number of rooms.

Code for This Project:

```python
from sklearn.datasets import fetch_california_housing
from sklearn.model_selection import train_test_split
from sklearn.linear_model import LinearRegression
from sklearn.metrics import mean_squared_error

# Load dataset
data = fetch_california_housing()
X, y = data.data, data.target

# Split data into training and testing sets
X_train, X_test, y_train, y_test = train_test_split(X,
y, test_size=0.2, random_state=42)

# Initialize and train the model
model = LinearRegression()
model.fit(X_train, y_train)

# Make predictions
y_pred = model.predict(X_test)

# Evaluate the model
error = mean_squared_error(y_test, y_pred)
print("Mean Squared Error:", error)

# Display coefficients
print("Model Coefficients:", model.coef_)
```

Expected Output:

- Mean Squared Error indicating model performance.
- Coefficients showing the influence of each feature on the target variable.

Chapter-11 Logistic Regression for Classification

This chapter introduces logistic regression, a widely-used algorithm for classification tasks, implemented with Scikit-learn. Logistic regression predicts probabilities for discrete class labels, making it suitable for binary and multi-class classification problems.

Key Characteristics of Logistic Regression:

- **Classification Model:** Predicts discrete class labels such as 0 or 1.
- **Probabilistic Approach:** Outputs probabilities for class membership.
- **Linear Decision Boundary:** Separates classes using a linear hyperplane.
- **Regularization:** Prevents overfitting with penalties such as L1 or L2.
- **Scalability:** Efficient for small to medium-sized datasets.

Basic Rules for Logistic Regression:

- Ensure the relationship between features and the log-odds of the target is approximately linear.
- Scale features to improve convergence and interpretability.
- Use regularization to avoid overfitting, especially with high-dimensional data.
- Evaluate the model using appropriate metrics such as accuracy, precision, recall, and F1-score.

Syntax Table:

SL No	Function	Syntax/Example	Description
1	Initialize Model	`LogisticRegression()`	Creates a logistic regression model instance.
2	Train Model	`model.fit(X_train, y_train)`	Fits the model to the training data.
3	Predict Outcomes	`model.predict(X_test)`	Predicts class labels for test data.
4	Predict	`model.predict_p`	Outputs class

	Probabilities	`roba(X_test)`	probabilities.
5	Evaluate Model	`accuracy_score( y_test, y_pred)`	Calculates the accuracy of predictions.

Syntax Explanation:

1. Initialize Model

What is Initializing a Logistic Regression Model?
Creates an instance of the logistic regression model.
Syntax:
```
from sklearn.linear_model import LogisticRegression
model = LogisticRegression()
```

Syntax Explanation:
- `LogisticRegression()`: Initializes the model with default settings.
    - Includes parameters for regularization:
        - penalty: Specifies the regularization type (`'l1'`, `'l2'`, `'elasticnet'`, or `'none'`).
        - C: Inverse of regularization strength (smaller values = stronger regularization).
    - Default solver is `'lbfgs'`, suitable for most datasets.
- Prepares the model for training and prediction.

Example:
```
from sklearn.linear_model import LogisticRegression
model = LogisticRegression()
```

Example Explanation:
- Creates a logistic regression model ready for training.

2. Train Model

What is Training a Logistic Regression Model?
Fits the model to the training data by finding parameters that maximize the likelihood of correct predictions.
Syntax:

```
model.fit(X_train, y_train)
```

Syntax Explanation:
- `fit(X_train, y_train)`: Uses the training features
  (`X_train`) and corresponding target labels (`y_train`) to learn
  the model parameters.
  - Maximizes the log-likelihood function to separate classes.
  - Handles binary and multi-class targets automatically.

Example:
```
import numpy as np
from sklearn.linear_model import LogisticRegression

X_train = np.random.rand(100, 5)    # 100 samples, 5
features
y_train = np.random.randint(0, 2, 100)    # Binary target
model = LogisticRegression()
model.fit(X_train, y_train)
```

Example Explanation:
- Trains a logistic regression model on randomly generated data.
- Learns coefficients and intercept to separate classes.

3. Predict Outcomes

What is Predicting Outcomes?
Generates class labels for new data based on the trained model.
Syntax:
```
y_pred = model.predict(X_test)
```
Syntax Explanation:
- `predict(X_test)`: Uses the trained model to assign class labels
  (0, 1, etc.) to input features.
  - Applies a threshold of 0.5 by default to determine class
    membership.

Example:
```
X_test = np.random.rand(20, 5)    # 20 samples, 5
features
y_pred = model.predict(X_test)
```

```
print("Predicted Labels:", y_pred)
```
Example Explanation:
- Predicts binary class labels for test data.

4. Predict Probabilities

What is Predicting Probabilities?
Outputs the probability of each class for input data.
Syntax:
```
proba = model.predict_proba(X_test)
```
Syntax Explanation:
- `predict_proba(X_test)`: Returns an array of probabilities for
  each class.
    - For binary classification, each row contains two
      probabilities: `[P(class 0), P(class 1)]`.
    - The class with the highest probability is the predicted
      label.

Example:
```
proba = model.predict_proba(X_test)
print("Class Probabilities:\n", proba)
```
Example Explanation:
- Outputs probabilities such as `[[0.7, 0.3], [0.2, 0.8],
  ...]`, indicating the model's confidence in each class.

5. Evaluate Model

What is Model Evaluation?
Measures the model's performance using metrics such as accuracy.
Syntax:
```
from sklearn.metrics import accuracy_score
accuracy = accuracy_score(y_test, y_pred)
```

Syntax Explanation:
- `accuracy_score(y_test, y_pred)`: Compares predicted
  labels with true labels and calculates the proportion of correct
  predictions.
- Suitable for balanced datasets; for imbalanced datasets, consider
```
```

precision, recall, or F1-score.

Example:
```
from sklearn.metrics import accuracy_score

y_test = np.random.randint(0, 2, 20)
accuracy = accuracy_score(y_test, y_pred)
print("Accuracy:", accuracy)
```

Example Explanation:
- Calculates the accuracy of predictions compared to true labels.

Real-Life Project:

Project Name: Spam Email Classification

Project Goal:

Train a logistic regression model to classify emails as spam or non-spam based on features such as word frequency and email metadata.

Code for This Project:

```
from sklearn.datasets import make_classification
from sklearn.model_selection import train_test_split
from sklearn.linear_model import LogisticRegression
from sklearn.metrics import accuracy_score,
classification_report

# Generate synthetic dataset
X, y = make_classification(n_samples=1000,
n_features=10, random_state=42)

# Split into training and testing sets
X_train, X_test, y_train, y_test = train_test_split(X,
y, test_size=0.2, random_state=42)

# Initialize and train logistic regression model
model = LogisticRegression()
model.fit(X_train, y_train)
```

```
# Make predictions
y_pred = model.predict(X_test)

# Evaluate the model
accuracy = accuracy_score(y_test, y_pred)
print("Accuracy:", accuracy)
print("Classification Report:\n",
classification_report(y_test, y_pred))
```

Expected Output:
- Outputs the accuracy of the logistic regression model.
- Provides a detailed classification report with precision, recall, and F1-score for each class.

Chapter-12 Decision Trees and Random Forests

This chapter introduces decision trees and random forests, two versatile and powerful algorithms for classification and regression tasks. Decision trees split data based on feature values to create a tree structure, while random forests enhance performance by combining multiple decision trees.

Key Characteristics of Decision Trees and Random Forests:

- **Interpretability:** Decision trees provide clear, human-readable rules.
- **Flexibility:** Handle classification and regression tasks.
- **Non-Parametric:** No assumptions about data distribution.
- **Random Forests:** Enhance decision trees by reducing overfitting and improving generalization.
- **Scalability:** Efficient for large datasets with many features.

Basic Rules for Decision Trees and Random Forests:

- Use decision trees for simple, interpretable models.
- Use random forests for robust, high-performing models on complex datasets.
- Avoid overfitting by tuning hyperparameters such as tree depth or the number of trees.
- Scale data when using random forests with distance-based metrics.
- Evaluate performance with metrics like accuracy, precision, and F1-score.

Syntax Table:

SL No	Function	Syntax/Example	Description
1	Decision Tree Classifier	DecisionTree Classifier()	Creates a decision tree classifier instance.
2	Decision Tree Regressor	DecisionTree Regressor()	Creates a decision tree regressor instance.

3	Random Forest Classifier	`RandomForest Classifier()`	Initializes a random forest for classification.
4	Random Forest Regressor	`RandomForest Regressor()`	Initializes a random forest for regression.
5	Feature Importance	`model.featur e_importance s_`	Displays the importance of each feature.

Syntax Explanation:

1. Decision Tree Classifier

What is a Decision Tree Classifier?
Predicts class labels by splitting data based on feature values into a tree structure.

Syntax:
```
from sklearn.tree import DecisionTreeClassifier
model = DecisionTreeClassifier()
```

Syntax Explanation:
- `DecisionTreeClassifier()`: Initializes a classification tree.
  - Key hyperparameters include:
    - `criterion`: The metric for splitting (`'gini'` or `'entropy'`).
    - `max_depth`: Maximum depth of the tree to control overfitting.
    - `min_samples_split`: Minimum samples required to split a node.
- Prepares the model for training and prediction.

Example:
```
from sklearn.tree import DecisionTreeClassifier
import numpy as np

X = np.random.rand(100, 4)  # 100 samples, 4 features
y = np.random.randint(0, 2, 100)  # Binary target
model = DecisionTreeClassifier(max_depth=3)
model.fit(X, y)
```
Example Explanation:

- Fits a decision tree with a maximum depth of 3 on the dataset.
- Learns decision rules to separate classes.

2. Decision Tree Regressor

What is a Decision Tree Regressor?
Predicts continuous target values by splitting data into regions based on feature values.

Syntax:
```
from sklearn.tree import DecisionTreeRegressor
model = DecisionTreeRegressor()
```
Syntax Explanation:
- `DecisionTreeRegressor()`: Initializes a regression tree.
  - Key hyperparameters include:
    - `criterion`: Metric for splitting (`'squared_error'` or `'friedman_mse'`).
    - `max_depth, min_samples_split`: Control tree complexity.
- Suitable for datasets with continuous target variables.

Example:
```
from sklearn.tree import DecisionTreeRegressor
import numpy as np

X = np.random.rand(100, 3)  # 100 samples, 3 features
y = np.random.rand(100)  # Continuous target
model = DecisionTreeRegressor(max_depth=4)
model.fit(X, y)
```
Example Explanation:
- Trains a decision tree to predict continuous target values.
- Outputs predictions based on the tree's splits.

3. Random Forest Classifier

What is a Random Forest Classifier?
Ensemble of decision trees that combine predictions to improve accuracy and robustness.

Syntax:

```
from sklearn.ensemble import RandomForestClassifier
model = RandomForestClassifier()
```

Syntax Explanation:

- RandomForestClassifier(): Initializes a forest of decision trees for classification.
    - Key hyperparameters include:
        - n_estimators: Number of trees in the forest.
        - max_features: Number of features to consider for splits.
        - bootstrap: Whether to use bootstrapped samples for training.
- Aggregates tree predictions using majority voting.

Example:

```
from sklearn.ensemble import RandomForestClassifier
import numpy as np


X = np.random.rand(200, 5)  # 200 samples, 5 features
y = np.random.randint(0, 2, 200)  # Binary target
model = RandomForestClassifier(n_estimators=100,
max_depth=5)
model.fit(X, y)
```

Example Explanation:

- Fits a random forest with 100 trees and a maximum depth of 5.
- Combines predictions from individual trees to classify samples.

4. Random Forest Regressor

What is a Random Forest Regressor?
Ensemble of decision trees that predict continuous values by averaging individual tree outputs.

Syntax:
```
from sklearn.ensemble import RandomForestRegressor
model = RandomForestRegressor()
```

Syntax Explanation:

- **RandomForestRegressor()**: Initializes a random forest for regression.
  - Key hyperparameters include:
    - n_estimators, max_features, and max_depth.
- Reduces variance by averaging predictions from multiple trees.

Example:

```
from sklearn.ensemble import RandomForestRegressor
import numpy as np


X = np.random.rand(150, 6)   # 150 samples, 6 features
y = np.random.rand(150)   # Continuous target
model = RandomForestRegressor(n_estimators=50,
max_depth=7)
model.fit(X, y)
```

Example Explanation:
- Trains a random forest with 50 trees for regression tasks.
- Outputs averaged predictions to minimize errors.

5. Feature Importance

What is Feature Importance?
Indicates the significance of each feature in the model's predictions.
Syntax:
```
importances = model.feature_importances_
```

Syntax Explanation:
- feature_importances_: Array of feature importance scores.
  - Higher values indicate greater influence on the target variable.
- Helps identify relevant features for the model.

Example:
```
importances = model.feature_importances_
print("Feature Importances:", importances)
```

Example Explanation:

- Outputs a list of importance scores for each feature.
- Useful for feature selection or understanding model behavior.

Real-Life Project:

Project Name: Predicting Customer Churn

Project Goal:

Build a random forest classifier to predict customer churn based on demographic and usage data.

Code for This Project:

```python
from sklearn.datasets import make_classification
from sklearn.model_selection import train_test_split
from sklearn.ensemble import RandomForestClassifier
from sklearn.metrics import accuracy_score

# Generate synthetic dataset
X, y = make_classification(n_samples=1000,
n_features=10, random_state=42)

# Split into training and testing sets
X_train, X_test, y_train, y_test = train_test_split(X,
y, test_size=0.2, random_state=42)

# Train random forest classifier
model = RandomForestClassifier(n_estimators=100,
max_depth=8)
model.fit(X_train, y_train)

# Make predictions
y_pred = model.predict(X_test)
# Evaluate model
accuracy = accuracy_score(y_test, y_pred)
print("Accuracy:", accuracy)
# Feature importance
print("Feature Importances:",
model.feature_importances_)
```

Expected Output:

- Accuracy of the random forest model.
- Feature importance scores for understanding influential features.

Chapter-13 Support Vector Machines (SVMs)

This chapter delves into Support Vector Machines (SVMs), a powerful and versatile algorithm for classification, regression, and outlier detection tasks. SVMs work by finding the hyperplane that best separates data points from different classes.

Key Characteristics of SVMs:

- **Hyperplane-Based:** Separates classes using a hyperplane with the largest margin.
- **Kernel Trick:** Maps data to higher dimensions to handle non-linear separations.
- **Robustness:** Effective in high-dimensional spaces and resistant to overfitting.
- **Versatility:** Supports classification, regression (SVR), and one-class SVMs for anomaly detection.
- **Scalability:** Efficient for medium-sized datasets.

Basic Rules for SVMs:

- Choose the appropriate kernel (linear, polynomial, RBF, etc.) for the problem.
- Scale features to ensure better performance and faster convergence.
- Use regularization to balance margin maximization and misclassification.
- Optimize hyperparameters (e.g., C, gamma) using cross-validation.
- Evaluate performance with metrics like accuracy, precision, and recall.

Syntax Table:

SL No	Function	Syntax/Example	Description
1	SVM Classifier	`SVC(kernel='li near')`	Creates an SVM classifier instance.
2	SVM	`SVR(kernel='rb`	Creates an SVM regressor

		f')	instance.
3	Train Model	`model.fit(X_tr ain, y_train)`	Fits the SVM to the training data.
4	Predict Outcomes	`model.predict( X_test)`	Predicts class labels or target values.
5	Kernel Customizatio n	`SVC(kernel='po ly', degree=3)`	Applies a polynomial kernel of degree 3.

Syntax Explanation:

1. SVM Classifier

What is an SVM Classifier?
An SVM classifier separates data into classes using a hyperplane that maximizes the margin between class boundaries.

Syntax:
```
from sklearn.svm import SVC
model = SVC(kernel='linear')
```
Syntax Explanation:
- SVC( ): Initializes an SVM classifier.
    - kernel: Specifies the kernel type (e.g., 'linear', 'poly', 'rbf', 'sigmoid').
    - C: Regularization parameter; smaller values create a wider margin but allow more misclassifications.
    - gamma: Controls the influence of a single data point (used in non-linear kernels).
- Prepares the model for training and prediction.

Example:
```
from sklearn.svm import SVC
import numpy as np

X = np.random.rand(100, 2)  # 100 samples, 2 features
y = np.random.randint(0, 2, 100)  # Binary target
model = SVC(kernel='linear')
model.fit(X, y)
```
Example Explanation:

- Fits an SVM classifier with a linear kernel to the dataset.
- Learns a decision boundary that separates the two classes.

2. SVM Regressor

What is an SVM Regressor?
An SVM regressor predicts continuous values by finding a hyperplane that minimizes the prediction error within a margin.

Syntax:
```
from sklearn.svm import SVR
model = SVR(kernel='rbf')
```

Syntax Explanation:
- SVR(): Initializes an SVM for regression.
    - kernel: Specifies the kernel function.
    - C: Regularization parameter balancing margin width and error tolerance.
    - epsilon: Specifies the margin of tolerance around the hyperplane where no penalty is given.

Example:
```
from sklearn.svm import SVR
import numpy as np

X = np.random.rand(100, 1)  # 100 samples, 1 feature
y = np.random.rand(100)  # Continuous target
model = SVR(kernel='rbf', C=1.0, epsilon=0.1)
model.fit(X, y)
```

Example Explanation:
- Fits an SVM regressor with an RBF kernel to the dataset.
- Learns a smooth curve to predict continuous values.

3. Train Model

What is Training an SVM?
Fitting an SVM involves finding the optimal hyperplane or curve that minimizes error while separating classes or predicting values.

Syntax:

```
model.fit(X_train, y_train)
```

Syntax Explanation:
- `fit(X_train, y_train)`: Uses the training data (`X_train`) and labels (`y_train`) to learn the hyperplane or curve.
- Finds support vectors that define the decision boundary.

Example:
```
from sklearn.svm import SVC
import numpy as np

X_train = np.random.rand(80, 2)
y_train = np.random.randint(0, 2, 80)
model = SVC(kernel='rbf')
model.fit(X_train, y_train)
```

Example Explanation:
- Fits an SVM classifier with an RBF kernel to the training data.
- Optimizes the decision boundary using support vectors.

4. Predict Outcomes

What is Predicting Outcomes with SVM?
Generates class labels or predicted values for new data.
Syntax:
```
y_pred = model.predict(X_test)
```

Syntax Explanation:
- `predict(X_test)`: Uses the trained SVM model to predict labels (0, 1, etc.) or continuous values for input data.
- For classification, outputs class labels; for regression, outputs predicted values.

Example:
```
X_test = np.random.rand(20, 2)
y_pred = model.predict(X_test)
print("Predictions:", y_pred)
```

Example Explanation:
- Predicts class labels for the test data using the trained SVM model.

5. Kernel Customization

What is Kernel Customization?
Specifies the kernel function for the SVM, which defines how data is mapped into higher dimensions.

Syntax:
```
model = SVC(kernel='poly', degree=3)
```

Syntax Explanation:
- kernel: Specifies the kernel type ('linear', 'poly', 'rbf', 'sigmoid').
- degree: Defines the degree of the polynomial kernel (used only with 'poly').
- gamma: Controls the kernel's influence on individual data points.

Example:
```
from sklearn.svm import SVC
model = SVC(kernel='poly', degree=3)
```

Example Explanation:
- Initializes an SVM classifier with a polynomial kernel of degree 3.
- Suitable for non-linear relationships.

Real-Life Project:

Project Name: Handwritten Digit Classification

Project Goal:
Train an SVM model to classify handwritten digits from the MNIST dataset.

Code for This Project:

```
from sklearn import datasets
from sklearn.model_selection import train_test_split
from sklearn.svm import SVC
from sklearn.metrics import accuracy_score

# Load the dataset
digits = datasets.load_digits()
X, y = digits.data, digits.target
```

```python
# Split into training and testing sets
X_train, X_test, y_train, y_test = train_test_split(X,
y, test_size=0.2, random_state=42)

# Initialize and train SVM classifier
model = SVC(kernel='rbf', C=1.0, gamma=0.01)
model.fit(X_train, y_train)

# Make predictions
y_pred = model.predict(X_test)

# Evaluate the model
accuracy = accuracy_score(y_test, y_pred)
print("Accuracy:", accuracy)
```

Expected Output:

- Outputs the accuracy of the SVM model on the test set.
- Demonstrates effective classification of handwritten digits.

Chapter- 14 K-Nearest Neighbors (KNN) Algorithm

This chapter introduces the K-Nearest Neighbors (KNN) algorithm, a simple yet powerful method for classification and regression tasks. KNN works by comparing a new data point to its nearest neighbors in the feature space to make predictions.

Key Characteristics of KNN:

- **Instance-Based Learning:** Makes predictions based on the closest examples in the training dataset.
- **Non-Parametric:** No assumptions about the underlying data distribution.
- **Distance Metrics:** Uses metrics like Euclidean, Manhattan, or Minkowski distance to compute similarity.
- **Flexibility:** Supports both classification and regression tasks.
- **Scalability:** Suitable for small to medium-sized datasets.

Basic Rules for KNN:

- Choose an appropriate value for k, the number of neighbors.
- Scale features to ensure fair distance calculations.
- Use cross-validation to determine the best value of k.
- Opt for weighted voting for classification if neighbors have different proximities.
- Use efficient data structures (e.g., KD-Trees) for faster neighbor searches.

Syntax Table:

SL	Function	Syntax/Example	Description
1	KNN Classifier	`KNeighborsClassifier(n_neighbors=5)`	Initializes a KNN classifier with k=5.
2	KNN Regressor	`KNeighborsRegressor(n_neighbors=3)`	Initializes a KNN regressor with k=3.
3	Train Model	`model.fit(X_train, y_train)`	Fits the KNN model to the training data.
4	Predict Outcomes	`model.predict(X_test)`	Predicts class labels or target values.
5	Weighted	`weights='distance'`	Uses proximity-based

	Voting		weighting.

Syntax Explanation:

1. KNN Classifier

What is a KNN Classifier?
A KNN classifier predicts class labels for new data points by majority voting among the k nearest neighbors.
Syntax:
```
from sklearn.neighbors import KNeighborsClassifier
model = KNeighborsClassifier(n_neighbors=5)
```

Syntax Explanation:
- `KNeighborsClassifier(n_neighbors=5)`: Initializes a KNN classifier with 5 neighbors.
  - `n_neighbors`: Number of neighbors to consider for voting.
  - `weights`: Weighting scheme (`'uniform'` or `'distance'`).
  - `metric`: Distance metric for computing neighbors (e.g., `'euclidean'`, `'manhattan'`).
- Prepares the model for training and prediction.

Example:
```
from sklearn.neighbors import KNeighborsClassifier
import numpy as np

X_train = np.random.rand(100, 4)  # 100 samples, 4
features
y_train = np.random.randint(0, 3, 100)  # 3-class
target
model = KNeighborsClassifier(n_neighbors=5)
model.fit(X_train, y_train)
```

Example Explanation:
- Fits a KNN classifier with k=5 to the dataset.
- Uses the majority class among the nearest neighbors to predict

labels.

2. KNN Regressor

What is a KNN Regressor?

A KNN regressor predicts continuous values for new data points by averaging the values of the k nearest neighbors.

Syntax:

```
from sklearn.neighbors import KNeighborsRegressor
model = KNeighborsRegressor(n_neighbors=3)
```

Syntax Explanation:

- `KNeighborsRegressor(n_neighbors=3)`: Initializes a KNN regressor with 3 neighbors.
    - `n_neighbors`: Number of neighbors to average for predictions.
    - `weights`: Specifies how neighbors contribute to predictions (`'uniform'` or `'distance'`).
- Suitable for regression tasks where the target variable is continuous.

Example:

```
from sklearn.neighbors import KNeighborsRegressor
import numpy as np

X_train = np.random.rand(100, 2)  # 100 samples, 2 features
y_train = np.random.rand(100)  # Continuous target
model = KNeighborsRegressor(n_neighbors=3)
model.fit(X_train, y_train)
```

Example Explanation:

- Fits a KNN regressor with k=3 to the dataset.
- Predicts target values by averaging the values of the nearest neighbors.

3. Train Model

What is Training a KNN Model?

Training a KNN model involves storing the training data for later use during predictions.

Syntax:

```
model.fit(X_train, y_train)
```

Syntax Explanation:

- `fit(X_train, y_train)`: Stores the training features (X_train) and labels (y_train) in memory.
- KNN does not build an explicit model but uses the stored data for neighbor searches.

Example:

```
X_train = np.random.rand(80, 3)
y_train = np.random.randint(0, 2, 80)
model.fit(X_train, y_train)
```

Example Explanation:

- Stores the training dataset for future neighbor-based predictions.

4. Predict Outcomes

What is Predicting Outcomes with KNN?

Uses the nearest neighbors to predict class labels (classification) or target values (regression) for new data points.

Syntax:

```
y_pred = model.predict(X_test)
```

Syntax Explanation:

- `predict(X_test)`: Computes predictions for the test data (X_test) based on the stored training data.
    - For classification, predicts the majority class among neighbors.
    - For regression, predicts the average target value of neighbors.

Example:

```
X_test = np.random.rand(20, 3)
y_pred = model.predict(X_test)
print("Predictions:", y_pred)
```

Example Explanation:

- Predicts class labels or continuous values for test samples using the trained KNN model.

5. Weighted Voting

What is Weighted Voting in KNN?
In weighted voting, neighbors closer to the query point have a higher influence on the prediction.

Syntax:
```
model = KNeighborsClassifier(n_neighbors=5,
weights='distance')
```

Syntax Explanation:
- `weights='distance'`: Neighbors are weighted inversely proportional to their distance.
- Reduces the influence of distant neighbors, improving predictions for non-uniform data distributions.

Example:
```
model = KNeighborsClassifier(n_neighbors=5,
weights='distance')
```

Example Explanation:
- Initializes a KNN classifier with weighted voting based on distances.
- Prioritizes closer neighbors when making predictions.

Real-Life Project:

Project Name: Predicting Wine Quality

Project Goal:
Build a KNN model to classify wine samples as high or low quality based on chemical properties.

Code for This Project:

```python
from sklearn.datasets import load_wine
from sklearn.model_selection import train_test_split
from sklearn.neighbors import KNeighborsClassifier
from sklearn.metrics import accuracy_score

# Load dataset
data = load_wine()
X, y = data.data, data.target

# Split into training and testing sets
X_train, X_test, y_train, y_test = train_test_split(X,
y, test_size=0.2, random_state=42)

# Initialize and train KNN classifier
model = KNeighborsClassifier(n_neighbors=5)
model.fit(X_train, y_train)

# Make predictions
y_pred = model.predict(X_test)

# Evaluate model
accuracy = accuracy_score(y_test, y_pred)
print("Accuracy:", accuracy)
```

Expected Output:

- Outputs the accuracy of the KNN model on the test set.
- Demonstrates effective classification of wine samples using the KNN algorithm.

Chapter-15 Gradient Boosting and XGBoost

This chapter explores Gradient Boosting and XGBoost, two advanced machine learning techniques for classification and regression tasks. Gradient Boosting builds models iteratively by minimizing errors, while XGBoost extends Gradient Boosting with speed and performance optimizations.

Key Characteristics of Gradient Boosting and XGBoost:

- **Iterative Learning:** Builds models sequentially to correct errors of previous models.
- **Ensemble Approach:** Combines weak learners (usually decision trees) to create a strong model.
- **Flexibility:** Handles classification, regression, and ranking tasks.
- **Regularization:** Reduces overfitting through techniques like shrinkage and tree pruning.
- **Scalability (XGBoost):** Efficient for large datasets due to parallelization and hardware optimization.

Basic Rules for Gradient Boosting and XGBoost:

- Tune hyperparameters (e.g., learning rate, max depth) using cross-validation.
- Monitor performance metrics like accuracy or mean squared error to avoid overfitting.
- Use early stopping to halt training when performance stops improving.
- Scale features if using distance-based metrics in other components.

Syntax Table:

SL No	Function	Syntax/Example	Description
1	Gradient Boosting Regressor	`GradientBoostingRegressor()`	Initializes a Gradient Boosting regressor.

2	Gradient Boosting Classifier	`GradientBoost ingClassifier ()`	Initializes a Gradient Boosting classifier.
3	XGBoost Regressor	`XGBRegressor( )`	Initializes an XGBoost regressor.
4	XGBoost Classifier	`XGBClassifier ()`	Initializes an XGBoost classifier.
5	Feature Importance	`model.feature _importances_`	Displays feature importance scores.

Syntax Explanation:

1. Gradient Boosting Regressor

What is a Gradient Boosting Regressor?
A regression model that minimizes prediction errors by adding weak learners sequentially.

Syntax:
```
from sklearn.ensemble import GradientBoostingRegressor
model = GradientBoostingRegressor()
```

Syntax Explanation:
- `GradientBoostingRegressor()`: Initializes the model.
  - `n_estimators`: Number of boosting stages (default: 100).
  - `learning_rate`: Step size for updates (default: 0.1).
  - `max_depth`: Maximum depth of individual trees.
- Prepares the model for training and prediction.

Example:
```
from sklearn.ensemble import GradientBoostingRegressor
import numpy as np
X_train = np.random.rand(100, 3)
y_train = np.random.rand(100)
model = GradientBoostingRegressor(n_estimators=50,
learning_rate=0.1, max_depth=3)
model.fit(X_train, y_train)
```

Example Explanation:
- Trains a Gradient Boosting regressor with 50 trees, each of depth

3.

- Adjusts predictions iteratively to minimize errors.

2. Gradient Boosting Classifier

What is a Gradient Boosting Classifier?
A classification model that combines weak learners to improve prediction accuracy.

Syntax:
```
from sklearn.ensemble import GradientBoostingClassifier
model = GradientBoostingClassifier()
```

Syntax Explanation:
- `GradientBoostingClassifier()`: Initializes the model.
  - Similar parameters to `GradientBoostingRegressor`, with options for classification-specific tuning.

Example:
```
from sklearn.ensemble import GradientBoostingClassifier
import numpy as np

X_train = np.random.rand(100, 4)
y_train = np.random.randint(0, 2, 100)  # Binary target
model = GradientBoostingClassifier(n_estimators=100,
learning_rate=0.05, max_depth=4)
model.fit(X_train, y_train)
```

Example Explanation:
- Trains a Gradient Boosting classifier with 100 trees and a learning rate of 0.05.
- Corrects misclassified samples in each iteration.

3. XGBoost Regressor

What is an XGBoost Regressor?
A high-performance regression model that incorporates regularization, parallelization, and optimized algorithms.

Syntax:

```
from xgboost import XGBRegressor
model = XGBRegressor()
```

Syntax Explanation:
- XGBRegressor(): Initializes an XGBoost regressor.
  - n_estimators: Number of boosting rounds (default: 100).
  - learning_rate: Controls step size.
  - max_depth: Maximum depth of trees.
  - reg_alpha, reg_lambda: Regularization parameters to reduce overfitting.

Example:
```
from xgboost import XGBRegressor
import numpy as np

X_train = np.random.rand(150, 5)
y_train = np.random.rand(150)
model = XGBRegressor(n_estimators=200,
learning_rate=0.1, max_depth=4)
model.fit(X_train, y_train)
```

Example Explanation:
- Fits an XGBoost regressor with 200 boosting rounds and regularization.
- Uses parallelization for efficient computation.

4. XGBoost Classifier

What is an XGBoost Classifier?
A fast and scalable classifier that improves Gradient Boosting by leveraging hardware optimizations.

Syntax:
```
from xgboost import XGBClassifier
model = XGBClassifier()
```

Syntax Explanation:
- XGBClassifier(): Initializes an XGBoost classifier.
  - Similar parameters to XGBRegressor, with additional
```
```

settings for classification tasks.

Example:

```
from xgboost import XGBClassifier
import numpy as np

X_train = np.random.rand(200, 6)
y_train = np.random.randint(0, 3, 200)  # Multi-class
target
model = XGBClassifier(n_estimators=100,
learning_rate=0.2, max_depth=5)
model.fit(X_train, y_train)
```

Example Explanation:
- Trains an XGBoost classifier for a multi-class problem.
- Efficiently handles large feature spaces with optimized algorithms.

5. Feature Importance

What is Feature Importance in Gradient Boosting and XGBoost?
Provides scores for each feature, indicating its contribution to the model's predictions.
Syntax:
```
importances = model.feature_importances_
```

Syntax Explanation:
- `feature_importances_`: Array of importance scores for features.
    - Higher values indicate greater relevance to the model.
- Useful for feature selection and model interpretation.

Example:
```
importances = model.feature_importances_
print("Feature Importances:", importances)
```

Example Explanation:
- Outputs feature importance scores for understanding the impact of each feature.

Real-Life Project:

Project Name: Predicting Customer Loan Defaults

Project Goal:

Use XGBoost to predict loan defaults based on customer demographic and financial data.

Code for This Project:

```python
from xgboost import XGBClassifier
from sklearn.model_selection import train_test_split
from sklearn.metrics import accuracy_score,
classification_report
import numpy as np

# Generate synthetic dataset
X = np.random.rand(1000, 10)
y = np.random.randint(0, 2, 1000)  # Binary target
# Split into training and testing sets
X_train, X_test, y_train, y_test = train_test_split(X,
y, test_size=0.2, random_state=42)
# Train XGBoost classifier
model = XGBClassifier(n_estimators=100,
learning_rate=0.1, max_depth=6)
model.fit(X_train, y_train)
# Make predictions
y_pred = model.predict(X_test)
# Evaluate model
accuracy = accuracy_score(y_test, y_pred)
print("Accuracy:", accuracy)
print("Classification Report:\n",
classification_report(y_test, y_pred))
```

Expected Output:

- Outputs the accuracy of the XGBoost model.
- Provides a detailed classification report with precision, recall, and F1-score.

Chapter-16 Evaluating Supervised Learning Models

This chapter focuses on evaluating supervised learning models, a crucial step in understanding their performance and ensuring their effectiveness. Evaluation metrics provide insights into model accuracy, robustness, and reliability, allowing data scientists to fine-tune models for better outcomes.

Key Characteristics of Model Evaluation:

- **Quantitative Assessment:** Provides measurable metrics to compare model performance.
- **Task-Specific Metrics:** Different metrics for classification (e.g., accuracy) and regression (e.g., mean squared error).
- **Cross-Validation:** Ensures robust evaluation by testing models on multiple subsets of data.
- **Bias-Variance Tradeoff:** Balances overfitting and underfitting.
- **Interpretability:** Helps understand model strengths and weaknesses.

Basic Rules for Model Evaluation:

- Split data into training, validation, and testing subsets.
- Choose metrics that align with business goals and problem types.
- Use cross-validation for small datasets to maximize reliability.
- Regularly monitor metrics to avoid overfitting during training.
- Compare multiple models to identify the best-performing one.

Syntax Table:

SL No	Function	Syntax/Example	Description
1	Accuracy Score	accuracy_score(y _test, y_pred)	Measures overall correctness for classification.
2	Confusion Matrix	confusion_matrix (y_test, y_pred)	Displays true vs. predicted classifications.
3	Precision and	precision_score(	Evaluates positive class

	Recall	`y_test, y_pred)`	performance.
4	Mean Squared Error (MSE)	`mean_squared_err or(y_test, y_pred)`	Measures average squared errors in regression.
5	Cross-Validation Score	`cross_val_score( model, X, y)`	Computes scores for cross-validated splits.

Syntax Explanation:

1. Accuracy Score

What is Accuracy Score?
Accuracy score measures the proportion of correct predictions to the total number of predictions.

Syntax:
```
from sklearn.metrics import accuracy_score
accuracy = accuracy_score(y_test, y_pred)
```

Syntax Explanation:
- `accuracy_score(y_test, y_pred)`: Compares true labels (y_test) with predicted labels (y_pred) and calculates the ratio of correct predictions.
  - Best suited for balanced datasets.
  - Ignores class imbalance issues, so additional metrics may be needed for imbalanced data.

Example:
```
from sklearn.metrics import accuracy_score
import numpy as np

y_test = np.array([0, 1, 1, 0])
y_pred = np.array([0, 1, 0, 0])
accuracy = accuracy_score(y_test, y_pred)
print("Accuracy:", accuracy)
```

Example Explanation:
- Compares true labels [0, 1, 1, 0] with predicted labels [0, 1, 0, 0].

- Outputs an accuracy of 0.75, indicating 75% correctness.

2. Confusion Matrix

What is a Confusion Matrix?
A confusion matrix evaluates classification performance by showing true positives, true negatives, false positives, and false negatives.
Syntax:
```
from sklearn.metrics import confusion_matrix
matrix = confusion_matrix(y_test, y_pred)
```

Syntax Explanation:
- confusion_matrix(y_test, y_pred): Constructs a table that summarizes prediction outcomes.
    - Rows represent actual labels, and columns represent predicted labels.
    - Useful for calculating derived metrics like precision and recall.

Example:
```
from sklearn.metrics import confusion_matrix
import numpy as np

y_test = np.array([0, 1, 1, 0])
y_pred = np.array([0, 1, 0, 0])
matrix = confusion_matrix(y_test, y_pred)
print("Confusion Matrix:\n", matrix)
```

Example Explanation:
- Outputs: [[2 0]
        [1 1]]

- Indicates 2 true negatives, 1 false negative, and 1 true positive.

3. Precision and Recall

What are Precision and Recall?
Precision measures the accuracy of positive predictions, while recall

measures the proportion of actual positives correctly identified.

Syntax:

```
from sklearn.metrics import precision_score,
recall_score
precision = precision_score(y_test, y_pred)
recall = recall_score(y_test, y_pred)
```

Syntax Explanation:

- `precision_score`: Calculates the ratio of true positives to all predicted positives.
- `recall_score`: Calculates the ratio of true positives to all actual positives.
- Both metrics are crucial for imbalanced datasets.

Example:

```
from sklearn.metrics import precision_score,
recall_score
import numpy as np

y_test = np.array([0, 1, 1, 0])
y_pred = np.array([0, 1, 0, 0])
precision = precision_score(y_test, y_pred)
recall = recall_score(y_test, y_pred)
print("Precision:", precision)
print("Recall:", recall)
```

Example Explanation:

- Precision is `1.0`, indicating perfect accuracy among predicted positives.
- Recall is `0.5`, as only half of the actual positives were identified.

4. Mean Squared Error (MSE)

What is Mean Squared Error?

MSE measures the average squared differences between predicted and actual values in regression tasks.

Syntax:

```
from sklearn.metrics import mean_squared_error
mse = mean_squared_error(y_test, y_pred)
```

Syntax Explanation:

- `mean_squared_error(y_test, y_pred)`: Computes the average squared error between true values (`y_test`) and predictions (`y_pred`).
  - Penalizes larger errors more heavily than smaller ones.
- Lower values indicate better model performance.

Example:
```
from sklearn.metrics import mean_squared_error
import numpy as np

y_test = np.array([3.0, -0.5, 2.0, 7.0])
y_pred = np.array([2.5, 0.0, 2.0, 8.0])
mse = mean_squared_error(y_test, y_pred)
print("Mean Squared Error:", mse)
```

Example Explanation:

- Calculates an MSE of 0.375, indicating good model performance.

5. Cross-Validation Score

What is Cross-Validation?

Cross-validation evaluates a model's performance by testing it on multiple data splits.

Syntax:
```
from sklearn.model_selection import cross_val_score
scores = cross_val_score(model, X, y, cv=5)
```

Syntax Explanation:

- `cross_val_score`: Splits the dataset into cv subsets (default: 5) and evaluates the model on each.
  - Returns an array of scores, one for each split.
  - Ensures robust evaluation by reducing data-split bias.

Example:
```
from sklearn.model_selection import cross_val_score
from sklearn.linear_model import LogisticRegression
import numpy as np
```

```python
X = np.random.rand(100, 5)
y = np.random.randint(0, 2, 100)
model = LogisticRegression()
scores = cross_val_score(model, X, y, cv=5)
print("Cross-Validation Scores:", scores)
```

Example Explanation:

- Outputs scores like [0.85, 0.80, 0.90, 0.87, 0.83].
- Helps assess model consistency across different data splits.

Real-Life Project:

Project Name: Evaluating a Fraud Detection Model

Project Goal:

Assess a classification model's performance on imbalanced data using precision, recall, and F1-score.

Code for This Project:

```python
from sklearn.datasets import make_classification
from sklearn.model_selection import train_test_split
from sklearn.ensemble import RandomForestClassifier
from sklearn.metrics import classification_report
# Generate imbalanced dataset
X, y = make_classification(n_samples=1000,
n_features=10, weights=[0.9, 0.1], random_state=42)
# Split into training and testing sets
X_train, X_test, y_train, y_test = train_test_split(X,
y, test_size=0.2, random_state=42)
# Train model
model = RandomForestClassifier()
model.fit(X_train, y_train)
# Make predictions
y_pred = model.predict(X_test)
# Evaluate model
print("Classification Report:\n",
classification_report(y_test, y_pred))
```

Expected Output:

- Provides precision, recall, and F1-scores for both classes.
- Highlights performance on the minority class.

Chapter- 17 Introduction to Unsupervised Learning with Scikit-learn

This chapter introduces unsupervised learning, a machine learning approach that identifies patterns and structures in data without labeled outputs. Unsupervised learning algorithms are used for clustering, dimensionality reduction, and anomaly detection. Scikit-learn provides versatile tools for implementing these techniques efficiently.

Key Characteristics of Unsupervised Learning:

- **No Labels:** Operates on datasets without predefined labels.
- **Pattern Recognition:** Finds hidden structures, relationships, or groupings within data.
- **Scalability:** Suitable for analyzing large datasets.
- **Versatility:** Supports a variety of tasks, including clustering, association, and feature extraction.
- **Interpretation:** Provides insights into the underlying data distributions.

Basic Rules for Unsupervised Learning:

- Preprocess data by scaling or normalizing features to improve performance.
- Evaluate clustering with metrics like silhouette score, but note the lack of absolute benchmarks.
- Use dimensionality reduction techniques to visualize high-dimensional data.
- Select algorithms based on the dataset size, dimensionality, and task requirements.

Syntax Table:

SL No	Function	Syntax/Example	Description
1	K-Means Clustering	`KMeans(n_clusters=3)`	Partitions data into n clusters.
2	Hierarchical Clustering	`AgglomerativeClustering(n_cluste`	Groups data hierarchically.

		rs=2)	
3	Principal Component Analysis	PCA(n_components =2)	Reduces dimensionality of the dataset.
4	DBSCAN	DBSCAN(eps=0.5, min_samples=5)	Identifies clusters of varying shapes and sizes.
5	Feature Scaling	StandardScaler() .fit_transform(X)	Standardizes data for better performance.

Syntax Explanation:

1. K-Means Clustering

What is K-Means Clustering?
K-Means partitions data into a specified number of clusters by minimizing the sum of squared distances between points and their cluster centers.
Syntax:
```
from sklearn.cluster import KMeans
model = KMeans(n_clusters=3)
```

Syntax Explanation:
- KMeans(n_clusters=3): Initializes the algorithm with three clusters.
  - **n_clusters**: Defines the number of clusters to create.
  - **random_state**: Ensures reproducibility by setting a fixed seed for random number generation.
  - **max_iter**: The maximum number of iterations allowed for a single run of the algorithm.
  - **init**: Determines the method to initialize cluster centers (e.g., 'k-means++', 'random').
- Prepares the model for training by assigning initial cluster centers and optimizing their positions.

Example:
```
from sklearn.cluster import KMeans
import numpy as np
```

```
X = np.random.rand(100, 2)   # 100 samples, 2 features
model = KMeans(n_clusters=3, random_state=42)
model.fit(X)
```

Example Explanation:
- Divides the dataset into three clusters.
- Learns cluster centers and assigns each data point to the nearest cluster.

2. Hierarchical Clustering

What is Hierarchical Clustering?
Hierarchical clustering builds a tree-like structure of data points based on their similarities.

Syntax:
```
from sklearn.cluster import AgglomerativeClustering
model = AgglomerativeClustering(n_clusters=2)
```

Syntax Explanation:
- AgglomerativeClustering(n_clusters=2): Groups data into two clusters using a bottom-up approach.
    - linkage: Specifies the method to calculate distances between clusters ('ward', 'complete', 'average').
    - affinity: Metric to compute distances between points ('euclidean', 'manhattan', etc.).
    - Does not require specifying a random_state since the method is deterministic.
- Builds a dendrogram (hierarchical tree) by merging clusters iteratively until only the desired number of clusters remains.

Example:
```
from sklearn.cluster import AgglomerativeClustering
import numpy as np

X = np.random.rand(50, 2)   # 50 samples, 2 features
model = AgglomerativeClustering(n_clusters=2)
model.fit(X)
```

Example Explanation:

- Organizes data into a hierarchy, merging the closest data points first.
- Outputs cluster labels for each data point.

3. Principal Component Analysis (PCA)

What is PCA?

PCA reduces the dimensionality of data by projecting it onto a smaller number of components that capture the most variance.

Syntax:

```
from sklearn.decomposition import PCA
model = PCA(n_components=2)
```

Syntax Explanation:

- PCA(n_components=2): Reduces the dataset to two principal components.
  - **n_components**: Specifies the number of dimensions to retain.
  - Automatically sorts components by the amount of variance they explain.
  - Can handle datasets with highly correlated features by removing redundancy.

Example:

```
from sklearn.decomposition import PCA
import numpy as np

X = np.random.rand(100, 5)  # 100 samples, 5 features
model = PCA(n_components=2)
X_reduced = model.fit_transform(X)
```

Example Explanation:

- Projects the 5-dimensional data onto a 2-dimensional subspace while preserving as much variance as possible.

4. DBSCAN

What is DBSCAN?
Density-Based Spatial Clustering of Applications with Noise (DBSCAN) identifies clusters based on dense regions in the data.

Syntax:
```
from sklearn.cluster import DBSCAN
model = DBSCAN(eps=0.5, min_samples=5)
```

Syntax Explanation:
- DBSCAN(eps=0.5, min_samples=5): Identifies clusters where points are close to at least min_samples other points within a radius of eps.
  - **eps**: Maximum distance to consider points as part of the same cluster.
  - **min_samples**: Minimum number of points required to form a dense cluster.
  - Automatically identifies noise points that do not belong to any cluster.

Example:
```
from sklearn.cluster import DBSCAN
import numpy as np

X = np.random.rand(50, 2)  # 50 samples, 2 features
model = DBSCAN(eps=0.3, min_samples=4)
model.fit(X)
```

Example Explanation:
- Detects clusters of varying shapes and sizes.
- Marks outliers as noise points, which can be identified with model.labels_.

5. Feature Scaling

What is Feature Scaling?
Feature scaling standardizes data by centering it around the mean and scaling to unit variance.

Syntax:
```
from sklearn.preprocessing import StandardScaler
X_scaled = StandardScaler().fit_transform(X)
```

Syntax Explanation:
- StandardScaler().fit_transform(X): Scales each feature to have a mean of 0 and a standard deviation of 1.
    - Prevents features with larger ranges from dominating distance-based calculations.
    - Particularly useful for algorithms like K-Means and DBSCAN that rely on distances.

Example:
```
from sklearn.preprocessing import StandardScaler
import numpy as np

X = np.random.rand(50, 3)  # 50 samples, 3 features
X_scaled = StandardScaler().fit_transform(X)
```

Example Explanation:
- Standardizes the dataset, ensuring all features contribute equally to clustering.

Real-Life Project:
Project Name: Customer Segmentation for Retail
Project Goal:
Use clustering to segment customers based on purchase behavior, enabling targeted marketing strategies.

Code for This Project:

```
from sklearn.cluster import KMeans
from sklearn.preprocessing import StandardScaler
import numpy as np
```

```python
# Simulate customer purchase data
X = np.random.rand(200, 5)  # 200 customers, 5 purchase
features

# Scale the features
scaler = StandardScaler()
X_scaled = scaler.fit_transform(X)

# Apply K-Means clustering
model = KMeans(n_clusters=4, random_state=42)
model.fit(X_scaled)

# Cluster labels
labels = model.labels_
print("Cluster Labels:", labels)
```

Expected Output:

- Outputs cluster labels for each customer.
- Demonstrates effective customer segmentation using K-Means.

Chapter- 18 Linear Regression with Scikit-learn

This chapter explores linear regression, a fundamental algorithm in supervised learning, implemented using Scikit-learn. Linear regression models the relationship between input features and a continuous target variable by fitting a linear equation to the data.

Key Characteristics of Linear Regression:

- **Simple and Interpretable:** Easy to understand and interpret results.
- **Continuous Target Variable:** Predicts numeric outcomes (e.g., house prices).
- **Linearity Assumption:** Assumes a linear relationship between features and the target variable.
- **Optimization:** Uses Ordinary Least Squares (OLS) to minimize the error.
- **Scalability:** Efficient for small to medium-sized datasets.

Basic Rules for Linear Regression:

- Ensure the relationship between features and the target is approximately linear.
- Remove or address multicollinearity among features to improve model stability.
- Normalize or scale features if they differ in magnitude.
- Split data into training and testing subsets to evaluate model performance.

Syntax Table:

SL No	Function	Syntax/Example	Description
1	Initialize Model	`LinearRegression ()`	Creates a linear regression model instance.
2	Train Model	`model.fit(X_trai n, y_train)`	Fits the model to the training data.
3	Predict	`model.predict(X_`	Generates predictions for

	Outcomes	`test)`	input features.
4	Evaluate Model	`mean_squared_err or(y_test, y_pred)`	Calculates the error of predictions.
5	Get Coefficients	`model.coef_`	Retrieves the coefficients of the model.

Syntax Explanation:

1. Initialize Model

What is Initializing a Linear Regression Model?
Creates an instance of the linear regression model.
Syntax:
```
from sklearn.linear_model import LinearRegression
model = LinearRegression()
```

Syntax Explanation:
- `LinearRegression()`: Initializes the model with default settings for linear regression.
    - **`fit_intercept`**: When True (default), the model includes the intercept in the equation (e.g., `y = mx + b`). When `False`, the line passes through the origin.
    - **`normalize`**: Deprecated since Scikit-learn 0.24. If feature scaling is needed, use `StandardScaler` or other scaling tools.
    - **`n_jobs`**: Specifies the number of CPU cores to use for computation. By default, it uses a single core.
- Prepares the model for training by defining the parameters it will optimize.

Example:
```
from sklearn.linear_model import LinearRegression
model = LinearRegression()
```

Example Explanation:
- Creates a linear regression model ready to learn parameters such as coefficients and intercept from the training data.

2. Train Model

What is Training a Linear Regression Model?
Fits the model to the training data by finding the best-fit line that minimizes the sum of squared residuals.
Syntax:
```
model.fit(X_train, y_train)
```

Syntax Explanation:
- **fit(X_train, y_train):**
  - X_train: A 2D array where rows represent samples and columns represent features.
  - y_train: A 1D or 2D array of target values corresponding to X_train.
  - The method computes the slope (coefficients) and intercept that minimize the mean squared error between predicted and actual target values.
- This step updates the internal parameters of the model, which are stored in model.coef_ (coefficients) and model.intercept_ (intercept).

Example:
```
from sklearn.linear_model import LinearRegression
import numpy as np

X_train = np.array([[1], [2], [3], [4]])
y_train = np.array([2.5, 3.5, 4.5, 5.5])
model = LinearRegression()
model.fit(X_train, y_train)
```

Example Explanation:
- Fits the model to a simple dataset where X_train contains feature values, and y_train contains corresponding targets.
- Learns the relationship: y = 1 + x.
- The model stores the slope (coef_) and intercept (intercept_) for prediction.

3. Predict Outcomes

What is Predicting Outcomes?
Uses the trained model to predict target values for new input data.
Syntax:
```
y_pred = model.predict(X_test)
```

Syntax Explanation:
- **predict(X_test)**:
    - Takes X_test (a 2D array of test features) as input.
    - Computes predictions using the formula: `y_pred = intercept + sum(coefficients * features)`.
    - Returns an array of predicted target values (y_pred).

Example:
```
X_test = np.array([[5], [6]])
y_pred = model.predict(X_test)
print("Predictions:", y_pred)
```

Example Explanation:
- Uses the learned parameters to predict target values for X_test.
- Outputs predictions `[6.5, 7.5]` based on the relationship y = 1 + x.

4. Evaluate Model

What is Model Evaluation?
Quantifies the model's accuracy by comparing predictions with actual target values using evaluation metrics.
Syntax:
```
from sklearn.metrics import mean_squared_error
error = mean_squared_error(y_test, y_pred)
```

Syntax Explanation:
- **mean_squared_error(y_test, y_pred)**:
    - y_test: True target values.
    - y_pred: Predicted values from the model.
    - Computes the average of squared differences between

actual and predicted values. Smaller values indicate better
performance.
- o Sensitive to outliers, as larger errors contribute
disproportionately to the metric.

Example:
```
from sklearn.metrics import mean_squared_error
import numpy as np

y_test = np.array([6.5, 7.5])
y_pred = np.array([6.4, 7.6])
error = mean_squared_error(y_test, y_pred)
print("Mean Squared Error:", error)
```

Example Explanation:
- Compares true values [6.5, 7.5] with predictions [6.4,
7.6].
- Calculates the average squared error (0.01), reflecting the
model's accuracy.

5. Get Coefficients

What are Model Coefficients?
Model coefficients indicate the relationship between each feature and the
target variable in the linear equation.
Syntax:
```
coefficients = model.coef_
```

Syntax Explanation:
- **coef_**: A NumPy array containing the slopes (coefficients) of the
features.
  - o Each coefficient represents the change in the target
  variable for a one-unit change in the corresponding
  feature, assuming other features are constant.
- The intercept (intercept_) is the value of the target variable
when all features are zero.

Example:

```
coefficients = model.coef_
intercept = model.intercept_
print("Coefficients:", coefficients)
print("Intercept:", intercept)
```

Example Explanation:
- Outputs the coefficients and intercept:
  - Coefficients might be [1.0], indicating a one-to-one relationship with the feature.
  - Intercept might be 1.0, representing the value of y when x is zero.

Real-Life Project:

Project Name: Predicting House Prices

Project Goal:

Build a linear regression model to predict house prices based on features like size, location, and number of rooms.

Code for This Project:

```
from sklearn.datasets import fetch_california_housing
from sklearn.model_selection import train_test_split
from sklearn.linear_model import LinearRegression
from sklearn.metrics import mean_squared_error

# Load dataset
data = fetch_california_housing()
X, y = data.data, data.target

# Split data into training and testing sets
X_train, X_test, y_train, y_test = train_test_split(X,
y, test_size=0.2, random_state=42)

# Initialize and train the model
model = LinearRegression()
model.fit(X_train, y_train)
```

```python
# Make predictions
y_pred = model.predict(X_test)

# Evaluate the model
error = mean_squared_error(y_test, y_pred)
print("Mean Squared Error:", error)

# Display coefficients
print("Model Coefficients:", model.coef_)
```

Expected Output:

- Outputs the Mean Squared Error, indicating model performance.
- Displays coefficients for each feature, explaining their impact on the target variable.

Chapter-19 Logistic Regression for Classification

This chapter introduces logistic regression, a widely-used algorithm for classification tasks, implemented with Scikit-learn. Logistic regression predicts probabilities for discrete class labels, making it suitable for binary and multi-class classification problems.

Key Characteristics of Logistic Regression:

- **Classification Model:** Predicts discrete class labels such as 0 or 1.
- **Probabilistic Approach:** Outputs probabilities for class membership.
- **Linear Decision Boundary:** Separates classes using a linear hyperplane.
- **Regularization:** Prevents overfitting with penalties such as L1 or L2.
- **Scalability:** Efficient for small to medium-sized datasets.

Basic Rules for Logistic Regression:

- Choose the appropriate kernel (linear, polynomial, RBF, etc.) for the problem.
- Scale features to ensure better performance and faster convergence.
- Use regularization to balance margin maximization and misclassification.
- Optimize hyperparameters (e.g., C, gamma) using cross-validation.
- Evaluate performance with metrics like accuracy, precision, and recall.

Syntax Table:

SL No	Function	Syntax/Example	Description
1	Initialize Model	`LogisticRegression()`	Creates a logistic regression model instance.
2	Train Model	`model.fit(X_train, y_train)`	Fits the logistic regression model to the data.

3	Predict Class Labels	`model.predict(X_test)`	Predicts class labels for test data.
4	Predict Probabilities	`model.predict_proba(X_test)`	Outputs class probabilities for test data.
5	Evaluate Model	`accuracy_score(y_test, y_pred)`	Calculates the accuracy of the predictions.

Syntax Explanation:

1. Initialize Model

What is Initializing a Logistic Regression Model?
Creates an instance of a logistic regression model for binary or multi-class classification.
Syntax:
```
from sklearn.linear_model import LogisticRegression
model = LogisticRegression()
```
Syntax Explanation:
- **LogisticRegression()**: Initializes the logistic regression model.
    - **penalty**: Regularization type (`'l1'`, `'l2'`, `'elasticnet'`, or `'none'`).
    - **C**: Inverse of regularization strength (smaller values = stronger regularization).
    - **solver**: Optimization algorithm (`'lbfgs'`, `'liblinear'`, `'saga'`, etc.).
    - **multi_class**: Handles multi-class classification (`'auto'`, `'ovr'`, or `'multinomial'`).
- Prepares the model for training by defining its configuration.

Example:
```
from sklearn.linear_model import LogisticRegression
model = LogisticRegression(penalty='l2', C=1.0, solver='lbfgs')
```
Example Explanation:
- Initializes a logistic regression model with L2 regularization

(penalty='l2'), default regularization strength (C=1.0), and the 'lbfgs' solver.

2. Train Model

What is Training a Logistic Regression Model?
Fits the logistic regression model to the training data by learning the optimal weights and intercept that minimize the log-loss function. This process involves using optimization algorithms like gradient descent or variants depending on the specified solver.

Syntax:
```
model.fit(X_train, y_train)
```

Syntax Explanation:
- **fit(X_train, y_train):**
  - X_train: A 2D array of training features.
  - y_train: A 1D array of corresponding class labels.
  - Optimizes the model parameters (weights and intercept) using maximum likelihood estimation to minimize the log-loss function.

Example:
```
import numpy as np
from sklearn.linear_model import LogisticRegression

X_train = np.random.rand(100, 3)  # 100 samples, 3 features
y_train = np.random.randint(0, 2, 100)  # Binary classification
model = LogisticRegression()
model.fit(X_train, y_train)
```

Example Explanation:
- Fits the logistic regression model to the training dataset.
- Learns the weights for each feature and the intercept term.

3. Predict Class Labels

What is Predicting Class Labels?
Predicts class labels for new data points by utilizing the learned weights and bias from the training process. The model calculates probabilities for each class and assigns the label corresponding to the highest probability. This is particularly effective for binary or multi-class classification tasks.

Syntax:

```
y_pred = model.predict(X_test)
```

Syntax Explanation:
- **predict(X_test)**:
  - X_test: A 2D array of test features.
  - Uses the learned parameters to calculate the probability of each class and assigns the class with the highest probability as the predicted label.
  - Returns a 1D array of predicted class labels.

Example:

```
X_test = np.random.rand(20, 3)  # 20 samples, 3 features
y_pred = model.predict(X_test)
print("Predicted Labels:", y_pred)
```

Example Explanation:
- Predicts class labels (0 or 1) for the test data based on the trained model.

4. Predict Probabilities

What is Predicting Probabilities?
Calculates the probability of each class for new data points by applying the logistic function to the linear combination of the features and weights. This allows the model to express confidence in its predictions for each class, with probabilities summing to 1 across all classes for a given sample.

Syntax:

```
proba = model.predict_proba(X_test)
```

Syntax Explanation:
- **predict_proba(X_test)**:
  - Returns an array where each row contains the probabilities of each class for the corresponding test sample.
  - For binary classification, the two columns represent probabilities for classes 0 and 1.

Example:
```
proba = model.predict_proba(X_test)
print("Class Probabilities:\n", proba)
```

Example Explanation:
- Outputs probabilities such as `[[0.7, 0.3], [0.2, 0.8], ...]`, where each row sums to 1.

5. Evaluate Model

What is Model Evaluation?
Evaluates the model's performance by comparing predicted labels with true labels using metrics such as accuracy, precision, recall, and F1-score. Accuracy measures the proportion of correct predictions out of all predictions, providing an overall assessment of the model's correctness. For imbalanced datasets, additional metrics like recall and precision are crucial to ensure a comprehensive evaluation.

Syntax:
```
from sklearn.metrics import accuracy_score
accuracy = accuracy_score(y_test, y_pred)
```

Syntax Explanation:
- **accuracy_score(y_test, y_pred)**:
  - Compares the predicted labels (y_pred) with the true labels (y_test).
  - Calculates the proportion of correctly predicted samples.
  - Returns a scalar value representing the model's accuracy.

Example:
```
from sklearn.metrics import accuracy_score
```

```
y_test = np.random.randint(0, 2, 20)  # True labels
y_pred = np.random.randint(0, 2, 20)  # Predicted
labels
accuracy = accuracy_score(y_test, y_pred)
print("Accuracy:", accuracy)
```

Example Explanation:
- Calculates the accuracy of predictions compared to true labels.

Real-Life Project:

Project Name: Spam Email Classification

Project Goal:

Train a logistic regression model to classify emails as spam or non-spam based on features such as word frequency and email metadata.

Code for This Project:

```
from sklearn.datasets import make_classification
from sklearn.model_selection import train_test_split
from sklearn.linear_model import LogisticRegression
from sklearn.metrics import accuracy_score,
classification_report

# Generate synthetic dataset
X, y = make_classification(n_samples=1000,
n_features=10, random_state=42)

# Split into training and testing sets
X_train, X_test, y_train, y_test = train_test_split(X,
y, test_size=0.2, random_state=42)

# Train logistic regression model
model = LogisticRegression()
model.fit(X_train, y_train)

# Make predictions
y_pred = model.predict(X_test)
```

```
# Evaluate the model
accuracy = accuracy_score(y_test, y_pred)
print("Accuracy:", accuracy)
print("Classification Report:\n",
classification_report(y_test, y_pred))
```

Expected Output:

- Provides the accuracy of the logistic regression model.
- Outputs a detailed classification report with precision, recall, and
  F1-score for each class.

Chapter-20 Decision Trees and Random Forests

This chapter introduces decision trees and random forests, two powerful and versatile machine learning algorithms for classification and regression tasks. Decision trees split data based on feature values to create a tree-like structure, while random forests enhance performance by combining multiple decision trees in an ensemble approach.

Key Characteristics of Decision Trees and Random Forests:

- **Interpretability:** Decision trees provide a clear and human-readable set of rules.
- **Flexibility:** Suitable for both classification and regression tasks.
- **Non-Parametric:** No assumptions about the underlying data distribution.
- **Random Forests:** Use bagging and random feature selection to improve generalization.
- **Scalability:** Efficient for large datasets and high-dimensional data.

Basic Rules for Decision Trees and Random Forests:

- Use decision trees for simple, interpretable models.
- Use random forests for robust, high-performing models on complex datasets.
- Avoid overfitting by tuning hyperparameters like `max_depth` or `min_samples_split`.
- Use feature importance scores for insights into the most relevant features.
- Evaluate models with appropriate metrics like accuracy or mean squared error.

Syntax Table:

SL No	Function	Syntax/Example	Description
1	Decision Tree Classifier	`DecisionTree Classifier()`	Creates a decision tree for classification.
2	Decision Tree	`DecisionTree`	Creates a decision tree for

	Regressor	`Regressor()`	regression.
3	Random Forest Classifier	`RandomForest Classifier()`	Initializes a random forest for classification.
4	Random Forest Regressor	`RandomForest Regressor()`	Initializes a random forest for regression.
5	Feature Importance	`model.featur e_importance s_`	Displays the importance of each feature.

Syntax Explanation:

1. Decision Tree Classifier

What is a Decision Tree Classifier?

A decision tree classifier splits data into branches based on feature values to classify input data into predefined categories.

Syntax:

```
from sklearn.tree import DecisionTreeClassifier
model = DecisionTreeClassifier()
```

Syntax Explanation:

- **`DecisionTreeClassifier()`**: Initializes the classifier.
  - **`criterion`**: Specifies the function to measure the quality of a split (`'gini'` for Gini impurity or `'entropy'` for information gain).
  - **`max_depth`**: Limits the depth of the tree to prevent overfitting.
  - **`min_samples_split`**: Minimum number of samples required to split an internal node.
  - **`random_state`**: Ensures reproducibility by setting a seed.

Example:

```
from sklearn.tree import DecisionTreeClassifier
import numpy as np
X = np.random.rand(100, 4)   # 100 samples, 4 features
y = np.random.randint(0, 2, 100)   # Binary target
model = DecisionTreeClassifier(max_depth=3,
random_state=42)
model.fit(X, y)
```

Example Explanation:

- Creates a decision tree classifier with a maximum depth of 3.

- Trains the model on the dataset, learning decision rules to classify data.

2. Decision Tree Regressor

What is a Decision Tree Regressor?
A decision tree regressor predicts continuous values by partitioning data into regions based on feature values.

Syntax:
```
from sklearn.tree import DecisionTreeRegressor
model = DecisionTreeRegressor()
```

Syntax Explanation:
- **DecisionTreeRegressor()**: Initializes the regression tree.
  - **criterion**: Metric for evaluating split quality (e.g., 'squared_error' for mean squared error).
  - **max_depth, min_samples_split**: Same as in the classifier.

Example:
```
from sklearn.tree import DecisionTreeRegressor
import numpy as np

X = np.random.rand(100, 3)  # 100 samples, 3 features
y = np.random.rand(100)   # Continuous target
model = DecisionTreeRegressor(max_depth=4)
model.fit(X, y)
```

Example Explanation:
- Trains a regression tree with a maximum depth of 4 to predict continuous outcomes.

3. Random Forest Classifier

What is a Random Forest Classifier?
A random forest classifier is an ensemble of decision trees, combining their predictions to improve accuracy and robustness.

Syntax:
```
from sklearn.ensemble import RandomForestClassifier
```

```python
model = RandomForestClassifier()
```

Syntax Explanation:
- **RandomForestClassifier()**: Initializes a random forest model for classification.
    - **n_estimators**: Number of trees in the forest (default: 100).
    - **max_features**: Number of features to consider for splitting at each node.
    - **bootstrap**: Whether to use bootstrapped samples for training.

Example:
```
from sklearn.ensemble import RandomForestClassifier
import numpy as np


X = np.random.rand(200, 5)   # 200 samples, 5 features
y = np.random.randint(0, 2, 200)   # Binary target
model = RandomForestClassifier(n_estimators=100,
max_depth=5, random_state=42)
model.fit(X, y)
```

Example Explanation:
- Creates a random forest with 100 trees and a maximum depth of 5.
- Combines predictions from all trees to classify samples.

4. Random Forest Regressor

What is a Random Forest Regressor?
A random forest regressor predicts continuous values by averaging predictions from multiple decision trees.

Syntax:
```
from sklearn.ensemble import RandomForestRegressor
model = RandomForestRegressor()
```

Syntax Explanation:
- **RandomForestRegressor()**: Initializes the regression forest.
    - **n_estimators, max_features**, and **max_depth**: Same as in the classifier.

Example:

```
from sklearn.ensemble import RandomForestRegressor
import numpy as np

X = np.random.rand(150, 6)  # 150 samples, 6 features
y = np.random.rand(150)  # Continuous target
model = RandomForestRegressor(n_estimators=50,
max_depth=7)
model.fit(X, y)
```

Example Explanation:
- Creates a random forest with 50 trees and a maximum depth of 7.
- Predicts target values by averaging tree predictions.

5. Feature Importance

What is Feature Importance?
Indicates the contribution of each feature to the model's predictions.
Syntax:
```
importances = model.feature_importances_
```

Syntax Explanation:
- **feature_importances_**: Array of scores representing the importance of each feature.
  - Higher scores indicate greater influence on predictions.

Example:
```
importances = model.feature_importances_
print("Feature Importances:", importances)
```
Example Explanation:
- Displays feature importance scores, helping identify key predictors.

Real-Life Project:
Project Name: Customer Churn Prediction
Project Goal:

Use a random forest classifier to predict customer churn based on usage patterns, demographics, and subscription details.

Code for This Project:

```python
from sklearn.datasets import make_classification
from sklearn.model_selection import train_test_split
from sklearn.ensemble import RandomForestClassifier
from sklearn.metrics import accuracy_score

# Generate synthetic dataset
X, y = make_classification(n_samples=1000,
n_features=10, random_state=42)

# Split into training and testing sets
X_train, X_test, y_train, y_test = train_test_split(X,
y, test_size=0.2, random_state=42)

# Train random forest classifier
model = RandomForestClassifier(n_estimators=100,
max_depth=8, random_state=42)
model.fit(X_train, y_train)

# Make predictions
y_pred = model.predict(X_test)

# Evaluate model
accuracy = accuracy_score(y_test, y_pred)
print("Accuracy:", accuracy)

# Display feature importance
importances = model.feature_importances_
print("Feature Importances:", importances)
```

Expected Output:

- Displays the accuracy of the random forest model.
- Provides feature importance scores for interpretability.

Chapter-21 Support Vector Machines (SVMs)

This chapter explores Support Vector Machines (SVMs), a versatile and powerful algorithm for classification, regression, and outlier detection tasks. SVMs work by finding the hyperplane that best separates data points of different classes with the largest margin.

Key Characteristics of SVMs:

- **Hyperplane-Based:** Separates classes using a hyperplane that maximizes the margin.
- **Kernel Trick:** Handles non-linear relationships by mapping data into higher dimensions.
- **Robustness:** Effective in high-dimensional spaces and resistant to overfitting.
- **Flexibility:** Suitable for both classification and regression.
- **Customizability:** Offers parameters like C and gamma to control margin size and kernel behavior.

Basic Rules for SVMs:

- Scale features to avoid dominance of features with larger ranges.
- Use kernels like linear, polynomial, or RBF based on the data distribution.
- Optimize hyperparameters such as C and gamma using cross-validation.
- Handle imbalanced datasets by adjusting class weights.
- Evaluate model performance using metrics appropriate to the task, like accuracy or F1-score.

Syntax Table:

SL No	Function	Syntax/Example	Description
1	SVM Classifier	`SVC(kernel='linear')`	Creates an SVM classifier with a linear kernel.
2	SVM Regressor	`SVR(kernel='rbf')`	Creates an SVM regressor with an RBF kernel.
3	Train Model	`model.fit(X_train,`	Fits the SVM to the training data.

		y_train)	
4	Predict Outcomes	model.predict (X_test)	Predicts class labels or regression outputs.
5	Kernel Customizati on	SVC(kernel='p oly', degree=3)	Applies a polynomial kernel of degree 3.

Syntax Explanation:

1. SVM Classifier

What is an SVM Classifier?
An SVM classifier separates data into categories by finding the hyperplane that maximizes the margin between the classes.

Syntax:
```
from sklearn.svm import SVC
model = SVC(kernel='linear')
```

Syntax Explanation:
- **SVC(kernel='linear')**:
  - kernel: Specifies the kernel function (e.g., 'linear', 'poly', 'rbf', 'sigmoid').
  - C: Regularization parameter; smaller values create a wider margin but allow more misclassifications.
  - gamma: Controls the influence of individual data points in non-linear kernels.
- Initializes the model for classification tasks.

Example:
```
from sklearn.svm import SVC
import numpy as np

X = np.random.rand(100, 2)  # 100 samples, 2 features
y = np.random.randint(0, 2, 100)  # Binary target
model = SVC(kernel='linear', C=1.0)
model.fit(X, y)
```
Example Explanation:
- Trains an SVM classifier with a linear kernel on the dataset.

- Finds the optimal hyperplane to separate the two classes.

2. SVM Regressor

What is an SVM Regressor?
An SVM regressor predicts continuous values by finding a hyperplane that minimizes the error within a specified margin.
Syntax:
```
from sklearn.svm import SVR
model = SVR(kernel='rbf')
```

Syntax Explanation:
- **SVR(kernel='rbf')**:
    - kernel: Specifies the kernel function.
    - C: Regularization parameter controlling the trade-off between margin width and error tolerance.
    - epsilon: Defines a margin of tolerance where no penalty is given for errors.

Example:
```
from sklearn.svm import SVR
import numpy as np

X = np.random.rand(100, 1)  # 100 samples, 1 feature
y = np.random.rand(100)   # Continuous target
model = SVR(kernel='rbf', C=1.0, epsilon=0.1)
model.fit(X, y)
```

Example Explanation:
- Fits an SVM regressor with an RBF kernel to predict continuous outcomes.

3. Train Model

What is Training an SVM?
Fits the SVM to the data, optimizing the hyperplane or decision boundary for classification or regression tasks.
Syntax:

```
model.fit(X_train, y_train)
```

Syntax Explanation:
- **fit(X_train, y_train):**
  - ○ X_train: A 2D array of training features.
  - ○ y_train: A 1D array of target labels or values.
  - ○ Optimizes model parameters to minimize errors while maximizing the margin.

Example:
```
X_train = np.random.rand(80, 2)
y_train = np.random.randint(0, 2, 80)
model.fit(X_train, y_train)
```

Example Explanation:
- Trains the SVM using training data to learn decision boundaries or regression curves.

4. Predict Outcomes

What is Predicting Outcomes with SVM?
Uses the trained model to predict class labels or continuous values for new data.

Syntax:
```
y_pred = model.predict(X_test)
```

Syntax Explanation:
- **predict(X_test):**
  - ○ Takes X_test (a 2D array of test features) as input.
  - ○ For classification, predicts class labels (0, 1, etc.).
  - ○ For regression, predicts continuous target values.

Example:
```
X_test = np.random.rand(20, 2)
y_pred = model.predict(X_test)
print("Predictions:", y_pred)
```

Example Explanation:
- Predicts outcomes for test data using the trained model.

5. Kernel Customization

What is Kernel Customization?
Allows SVM to handle non-linear relationships by transforming input data into higher dimensions using kernel functions.

Syntax:
```
model = SVC(kernel='poly', degree=3)
```

Syntax Explanation:
- **kernel='poly':**
    - Specifies a polynomial kernel.
    - degree: Degree of the polynomial.
    - Useful for data with polynomial relationships.

Example:
```
model = SVC(kernel='poly', degree=3, C=1.0)
```

Example Explanation:
- Configures an SVM classifier with a polynomial kernel of degree 3.
- Maps data into higher dimensions for non-linear separations.

Real-Life Project:
Project Name: Handwritten Digit Classification
Project Goal:

Use SVM to classify handwritten digits from the MNIST dataset.

Code for This Project:

```
from sklearn.datasets import load_digits
from sklearn.model_selection import train_test_split
from sklearn.svm import SVC
from sklearn.metrics import accuracy_score

# Load dataset
digits = load_digits()
X, y = digits.data, digits.target
```

```
# Split into training and testing sets
X_train, X_test, y_train, y_test = train_test_split(X,
y, test_size=0.2, random_state=42)

# Initialize and train SVM classifier
model = SVC(kernel='rbf', C=1.0, gamma=0.01)
model.fit(X_train, y_train)

# Make predictions
y_pred = model.predict(X_test)

# Evaluate model
accuracy = accuracy_score(y_test, y_pred)
print("Accuracy:", accuracy)
```

Expected Output:

- Displays the accuracy of the SVM model on the test set.
- Demonstrates effective classification of handwritten digits.

Chapter-22 K-Nearest Neighbors (KNN) Algorithm

This chapter introduces the K-Nearest Neighbors (KNN) algorithm, a simple yet effective method for classification and regression tasks. KNN operates by identifying the closest data points (neighbors) to a given input and making predictions based on their values or labels.

Key Characteristics of KNN:

- **Instance-Based Learning:** Does not build an explicit model; predictions are made based on the training dataset.
- **Non-Parametric:** Makes no assumptions about the underlying data distribution.
- **Distance Metrics:** Relies on metrics like Euclidean, Manhattan, or Minkowski distance to find neighbors.
- **Flexibility:** Suitable for both classification and regression tasks.
- **Ease of Implementation:** Simple and intuitive algorithm.

Basic Rules for KNN:

- Choose an appropriate value of k (number of neighbors).
- Scale features to ensure fair distance calculations.
- Use a validation set or cross-validation to determine the optimal k.
- Weight neighbors based on their distance for improved accuracy.
- Efficiently handle larger datasets using optimized data structures like KD-Trees.

Syntax Table:

SL No	Function	Syntax/Example	Description
1	KNN Classifier	KNeighborsClassif ier(n_neighbors=5)	Initializes a KNN classifier with k=5.
2	KNN Regresso r	KNeighborsRegress or(n_neighbors=3)	Initializes a KNN regressor with k=3.

3	Train Model	`model.fit(X_train, y_train)`	Fits the KNN model to the training data.
4	Predict Outcomes	`model.predict(X_test)`	Predicts class labels or target values.
5	Weighted Voting	`weights='distance'`	Uses distance-based weighting for predictions.

Syntax Explanation:

1. KNN Classifier

What is a KNN Classifier?

A KNN classifier predicts class labels for new data points by considering the majority class among its k nearest neighbors.

Syntax:

```
from sklearn.neighbors import KNeighborsClassifier
model = KNeighborsClassifier(n_neighbors=5)
```

Syntax Explanation:

- **KNeighborsClassifier(n_neighbors=5):**
  - n_neighbors: Specifies the number of neighbors to consider for voting.
  - weights: Determines how neighbors contribute to predictions ('uniform' for equal weight, 'distance' for proximity-based weight).
  - metric: Defines the distance metric ('euclidean', 'manhattan', etc.).
- Prepares the classifier for training and prediction tasks.

Example:

```
from sklearn.neighbors import KNeighborsClassifier
import numpy as np
X_train = np.random.rand(100, 4)  # 100 samples, 4
features
y_train = np.random.randint(0, 2, 100)  # Binary target
model = KNeighborsClassifier(n_neighbors=5)
model.fit(X_train, y_train)
```

Example Explanation:

- Trains a KNN classifier with k=5 using the provided dataset.

- The classifier identifies the majority class among the 5 closest neighbors to make predictions.

2. KNN Regressor

What is a KNN Regressor?
A KNN regressor predicts continuous values by averaging the values of its k nearest neighbors.

Syntax:
```
from sklearn.neighbors import KNeighborsRegressor
model = KNeighborsRegressor(n_neighbors=3)
```

Syntax Explanation:
- **KNeighborsRegressor(n_neighbors=3):**
  - n_neighbors: Specifies the number of neighbors to consider for averaging.
  - weights: Determines how neighbors contribute to predictions ('uniform' or 'distance').
  - metric: Defines the distance metric.

Example:
```
from sklearn.neighbors import KNeighborsRegressor
import numpy as np

X_train = np.random.rand(100, 2)  # 100 samples, 2 features
y_train = np.random.rand(100)  # Continuous target
model = KNeighborsRegressor(n_neighbors=3)
model.fit(X_train, y_train)
```

Example Explanation:
- Trains a KNN regressor with k=3 to predict continuous outcomes by averaging the values of the nearest neighbors.

3. Train Model

What is Training a KNN Model?
Fits the KNN model to the training data by storing the dataset for use during predictions.

Syntax:
```
model.fit(X_train, y_train)
```

Syntax Explanation:

- **fit(X_train, y_train)**:
    - X_train: A 2D array containing training features.
    - y_train: A 1D array of corresponding target labels or values.
    - KNN stores the training data for neighbor-based predictions.

Example:
```
X_train = np.random.rand(80, 3)
y_train = np.random.randint(0, 2, 80)
model.fit(X_train, y_train)
```

Example Explanation:

- Stores the training data for use during neighbor searches.

4. Predict Outcomes

What is Predicting Outcomes with KNN?
Uses the stored training data to predict class labels or target values for new inputs.

Syntax:
```
y_pred = model.predict(X_test)
```

Syntax Explanation:

- **predict(X_test)**:
    - Takes X_test, a 2D array of test features, as input.
    - For classification, predicts the majority class among k nearest neighbors.
    - For regression, predicts the average target value of k nearest neighbors.

Example:
```
X_test = np.random.rand(20, 3)
y_pred = model.predict(X_test)
print("Predictions:", y_pred)
```

Example Explanation:
- Predicts class labels or target values for the test data.

5. Weighted Voting

What is Weighted Voting in KNN?
Assigns greater weight to closer neighbors, making their contribution to predictions more significant.
Syntax:
```
model = KNeighborsClassifier(n_neighbors=5,
weights='distance')
```

Syntax Explanation:
- **weights='distance':**
  - Neighbors closer to the input sample have more influence on the prediction.
  - Useful when closer neighbors are more likely to provide accurate information.

Example:
```
model = KNeighborsClassifier(n_neighbors=5,
weights='distance')
```

Example Explanation:
- Configures the classifier to use distance-based weighting for predictions.

Real-Life Project:
Project Name: Predicting House Prices
Project Goal:
Use KNN regression to predict house prices based on features like size, location, and number of rooms.

Code for This Project:

```
from sklearn.datasets import make_regression
from sklearn.model_selection import train_test_split
from sklearn.neighbors import KNeighborsRegressor
```

```python
from sklearn.metrics import mean_squared_error

# Generate synthetic dataset
X, y = make_regression(n_samples=200, n_features=3,
noise=0.1, random_state=42)

# Split into training and testing sets
X_train, X_test, y_train, y_test = train_test_split(X,
y, test_size=0.2, random_state=42)

# Train KNN regressor
model = KNeighborsRegressor(n_neighbors=5)
model.fit(X_train, y_train)

# Make predictions
y_pred = model.predict(X_test)

# Evaluate model
mse = mean_squared_error(y_test, y_pred)
print("Mean Squared Error:", mse)
```

Expected Output:

- Displays the mean squared error of the KNN regressor.
- Demonstrates effective regression using KNN.

Chapter-23 Gradient Boosting and XGBoost

This chapter introduces Gradient Boosting and XGBoost, two powerful machine learning techniques that improve predictive performance by iteratively correcting errors from previous models. Gradient Boosting builds models sequentially, while XGBoost extends Gradient Boosting with enhanced speed, scalability, and flexibility.

Key Characteristics of Gradient Boosting and XGBoost:

- **Sequential Learning:** Builds models in a step-by-step manner to reduce errors.
- **Ensemble Approach:** Combines weak learners (typically decision trees) to form a strong learner.
- **Customizability:** Offers various hyperparameters for fine-tuning (e.g., learning rate, max depth).
- **Regularization:** Prevents overfitting with techniques like shrinkage and tree pruning.
- **Efficiency (XGBoost):** Optimized for speed and scalability with parallel processing.

Basic Rules for Gradient Boosting and XGBoost:

- Use Gradient Boosting for general-purpose tasks and XGBoost for performance-critical applications.
- Tune hyperparameters (e.g., learning rate, number of trees) to improve model performance.
- Apply early stopping to avoid overfitting.
- Scale features if the dataset contains varying magnitudes.
- Monitor metrics like accuracy or RMSE during training for performance insights.

Syntax Table:

SL No	Function	Syntax/Example	Description
1	Gradient Boosting	`GradientBoostingRegr essor(n_estimators=1`	Initializes a Gradient Boosting

	Regressor	00)	regressor.
2	Gradient Boosting Classifier	`GradientBoostingClas sifier(n_estimators= 100)`	Initializes a Gradient Boosting classifier.
3	XGBoost Regressor	`XGBRegressor(n_estim ators=100, learning_rate=0.1)`	Initializes an XGBoost regressor.
4	XGBoost Classifier	`XGBClassifier(n_esti mators=100, learning_rate=0.1)`	Initializes an XGBoost classifier.
5	Feature Importance	`model.feature_import ances_`	Displays feature importance scores.

Syntax Explanation:

1. Gradient Boosting Regressor

What is a Gradient Boosting Regressor?
A Gradient Boosting regressor predicts continuous values by iteratively minimizing errors using weak learners.

Syntax:
```
from sklearn.ensemble import GradientBoostingRegressor
model = GradientBoostingRegressor(n_estimators=100,
learning_rate=0.1, max_depth=3)
```

Syntax Explanation:
- **`GradientBoostingRegressor(n_estimators=100, learning_rate=0.1, max_depth=3)`:**
    - `n_estimators`: Number of boosting stages.
    - `learning_rate`: Step size for weight updates (lower values = slower but more accurate training).
    - `max_depth`: Maximum depth of each tree.
- Combines weak learners to predict continuous target variables.

Example:
```
from sklearn.ensemble import GradientBoostingRegressor
import numpy as np
```

```
X_train = np.random.rand(100, 3)  # 100 samples, 3
features
y_train = np.random.rand(100)  # Continuous target
model = GradientBoostingRegressor(n_estimators=200,
learning_rate=0.05, max_depth=4)
model.fit(X_train, y_train)
```

Example Explanation:

- Fits a Gradient Boosting regressor with 200 trees, each having a depth of 4.
- Reduces errors at each stage by learning from residuals.

2. Gradient Boosting Classifier

What is a Gradient Boosting Classifier?
A Gradient Boosting classifier combines weak learners to classify input data into categories.

Syntax:
```
from sklearn.ensemble import GradientBoostingClassifier
model = GradientBoostingClassifier(n_estimators=100,
learning_rate=0.1, max_depth=3)
```

Syntax Explanation:

- **GradientBoostingClassifier(n_estimators=100, learning_rate=0.1, max_depth=3):**
  - Similar parameters to the regressor but adapted for classification tasks.

Example:
```
from sklearn.ensemble import GradientBoostingClassifier
import numpy as np

X_train = np.random.rand(100, 4)  # 100 samples, 4
features
y_train = np.random.randint(0, 2, 100)  # Binary target
model = GradientBoostingClassifier(n_estimators=150,
learning_rate=0.05, max_depth=3)
model.fit(X_train, y_train)
```

Example Explanation:
- Trains a Gradient Boosting classifier for binary classification.

3. XGBoost Regressor

What is an XGBoost Regressor?
An XGBoost regressor is an efficient and scalable version of Gradient Boosting for continuous target prediction.
Syntax:
```
from xgboost import XGBRegressor
model = XGBRegressor(n_estimators=100,
learning_rate=0.1, max_depth=3)
```

Syntax Explanation:
- **XGBRegressor(n_estimators=100, learning_rate=0.1, max_depth=3):**
    - Combines additional features like parallel processing and regularization.
    - Includes parameters for advanced optimization like subsample (fraction of samples for each tree).

Example:
```
from xgboost import XGBRegressor
import numpy as np

X_train = np.random.rand(200, 5)
y_train = np.random.rand(200)
model = XGBRegressor(n_estimators=200,
learning_rate=0.1, max_depth=5)
model.fit(X_train, y_train)
```

Example Explanation:
- Trains an XGBoost regressor for efficient prediction of continuous outcomes.

4. XGBoost Classifier

What is an XGBoost Classifier?

An XGBoost classifier predicts class labels using advanced boosting techniques.

Syntax:
```
from xgboost import XGBClassifier
model = XGBClassifier(n_estimators=100,
learning_rate=0.1, max_depth=3)
```

Syntax Explanation:
- **XGBClassifier(n_estimators=100, learning_rate=0.1, max_depth=3):**
  - Handles classification tasks with features for handling imbalance (e.g., scale_pos_weight).

Example:
```
from xgboost import XGBClassifier
import numpy as np
X_train = np.random.rand(300, 6)
y_train = np.random.randint(0, 3, 300)  # Multi-class
target
model = XGBClassifier(n_estimators=100,
learning_rate=0.2, max_depth=4)
model.fit(X_train, y_train)
```

Example Explanation:
- Trains an XGBoost classifier for a multi-class problem.

5. Feature Importance

What is Feature Importance in Boosting?

Provides insights into the contribution of each feature to the model's predictions.

Syntax:
```
importances = model.feature_importances_
```

Syntax Explanation:
- **feature_importances_**: Array of scores indicating the relevance of features in making predictions.

Example:
```
importances = model.feature_importances_
print("Feature Importances:", importances)
```

Example Explanation:

- Outputs a list of importance scores for understanding feature impact.

Real-Life Project:

Project Name: Predicting Loan Defaults

Project Goal:

Build an XGBoost model to predict loan defaults based on customer demographics and financial data.

Code for This Project:

```python
from xgboost import XGBClassifier
from sklearn.model_selection import train_test_split
from sklearn.metrics import accuracy_score,
classification_report
import numpy as np

# Simulated dataset
X = np.random.rand(1000, 10)
y = np.random.randint(0, 2, 1000)

# Split data
X_train, X_test, y_train, y_test = train_test_split(X,
y, test_size=0.2, random_state=42)
# Train XGBoost classifier
model = XGBClassifier(n_estimators=150,
learning_rate=0.1, max_depth=6)
model.fit(X_train, y_train)
# Make predictions
y_pred = model.predict(X_test)
# Evaluate performance
accuracy = accuracy_score(y_test, y_pred)
print("Accuracy:", accuracy)
print("Classification Report:\n",
classification_report(y_test, y_pred))
```

Expected Output:

- Outputs the accuracy of the XGBoost model.

- Provides a detailed classification report for performance evaluation.

Chapter-24 Evaluating Supervised Learning Models

This chapter covers the evaluation of supervised learning models, a crucial step to ensure their effectiveness and reliability. Proper evaluation provides insights into a model's performance, highlights areas for improvement, and ensures alignment with project goals. Common evaluation metrics vary depending on whether the task is classification or regression.

Key Characteristics of Model Evaluation:
- **Quantitative Analysis:** Provides numerical metrics for comparison.
- **Task-Specific Metrics:** Different metrics for classification (e.g., accuracy, F1-score) and regression (e.g., RMSE, R^2).
- **Robust Validation:** Includes techniques like cross-validation for reliability.
- **Bias-Variance Analysis:** Balances overfitting and underfitting.
- **Interpretability:** Metrics help identify model strengths and weaknesses.

Basic Rules for Model Evaluation:
- Split data into training, validation, and testing sets.
- Choose metrics relevant to the problem domain.
- Use cross-validation for robust performance estimates.
- Evaluate on unseen test data to measure generalization.
- Monitor metrics during training to detect overfitting.

Syntax Table:

SL No	Function	Syntax/Example	Description
1	Accuracy Score	`accuracy_score( y_test, y_pred)`	Measures correctness of predictions.
2	Confusion	`confusion_matri`	Displays true vs.

	Matrix	x(y_test, y_pred)	predicted classifications.
3	Mean Squared Error (MSE)	mean_squared_error(y_test, y_pred)	Computes average squared prediction errors.
4	R-Squared	r2_score(y_test, y_pred)	Measures variance explained by the model.
5	Cross-Validation Score	cross_val_score(model, X, y, cv=5)	Evaluates model across multiple data splits.

Syntax Explanation:

1. Accuracy Score

What is Accuracy Score?
Accuracy measures the ratio of correct predictions to the total number of predictions.
Syntax:
```
from sklearn.metrics import accuracy_score
accuracy = accuracy_score(y_test, y_pred)
```

Syntax Explanation:
- **accuracy_score(y_test, y_pred):**
  - ○ Compares true labels (y_test) with predicted labels (y_pred).
  - ○ Calculates the fraction of correct predictions.
- Best for balanced datasets; additional metrics may be needed for imbalanced datasets.

Example:
```
from sklearn.metrics import accuracy_score
import numpy as np

y_test = np.array([0, 1, 1, 0])
y_pred = np.array([0, 1, 0, 0])
accuracy = accuracy_score(y_test, y_pred)
print("Accuracy:", accuracy)
```

Example Explanation:
- Compares [0, 1, 1, 0] (true labels) with [0, 1, 0, 0] (predicted labels).
- Outputs 0.75, meaning 75% of predictions were correct.

2. Confusion Matrix

What is a Confusion Matrix?

A confusion matrix evaluates classification performance by showing true positives, true negatives, false positives, and false negatives.

Syntax:

```
from sklearn.metrics import confusion_matrix
matrix = confusion_matrix(y_test, y_pred)
```

Syntax Explanation:
- `confusion_matrix(y_test, y_pred)`:
  - Constructs a table summarizing prediction outcomes.
  - Rows represent actual labels; columns represent predicted labels.

Example:

```
from sklearn.metrics import confusion_matrix
import numpy as np

y_test = np.array([0, 1, 1, 0])
y_pred = np.array([0, 1, 0, 0])
matrix = confusion_matrix(y_test, y_pred)
print("Confusion Matrix:\n", matrix)
```

Example Explanation:
- Outputs: [[2 0]
  [1 1]]

- Indicates two true negatives, one false negative, and one true positive.

3. Mean Squared Error (MSE)

What is MSE?

MSE measures the average squared differences between predicted and true values in regression tasks.

Syntax:
```
from sklearn.metrics import mean_squared_error
mse = mean_squared_error(y_test, y_pred)
```

Syntax Explanation:
- **mean_squared_error(y_test, y_pred)**:
    - Computes the squared error for each prediction and averages the results.
    - Lower values indicate better model performance.

Example:
```
from sklearn.metrics import mean_squared_error
import numpy as np

y_test = np.array([3.0, -0.5, 2.0, 7.0])
y_pred = np.array([2.5, 0.0, 2.0, 8.0])
mse = mean_squared_error(y_test, y_pred)
print("Mean Squared Error:", mse)
```

Example Explanation:
- Calculates an MSE of 0.375, reflecting low prediction errors.

4. R-Squared

What is R-Squared?

R-squared measures how well a model explains the variability of the target variable.

Syntax:
```
from sklearn.metrics import r2_score
r2 = r2_score(y_test, y_pred)
```

Syntax Explanation:
- **r2_score(y_test, y_pred)**:
    - Calculates the proportion of variance explained by the model.
    - Values range from 0 to 1 (1 = perfect fit).

Example:

```
from sklearn.metrics import r2_score
import numpy as np
y_test = np.array([3.0, -0.5, 2.0, 7.0])
y_pred = np.array([2.5, 0.0, 2.0, 8.0])
r2 = r2_score(y_test, y_pred)
print("R-Squared:", r2)
```

Example Explanation:

- Outputs 0.948, indicating the model explains 94.8% of the variance.

5. Cross-Validation Score

What is Cross-Validation?
Cross-validation evaluates model performance by testing on multiple subsets of the data.

Syntax:
```
from sklearn.model_selection import cross_val_score
scores = cross_val_score(model, X, y, cv=5)
```

Syntax Explanation:

- **cross_val_score(model, X, y, cv=5):**
  - Splits the data into 5 subsets (folds).
  - Trains the model on 4 folds and tests on the remaining fold.
  - Repeats the process for all folds and averages the results.

Example:
```
from sklearn.model_selection import cross_val_score
from sklearn.linear_model import LinearRegression
import numpy as np

X = np.random.rand(100, 3)
y = np.random.rand(100)
model = LinearRegression()
scores = cross_val_score(model, X, y, cv=5)
print("Cross-Validation Scores:", scores)
```

Example Explanation:

- Outputs scores like `[0.85, 0.87, 0.90, 0.88, 0.84]`.
- Demonstrates model consistency across data splits.

Real-Life Project:

Project Name: Fraud Detection Model Evaluation

Project Goal:

Evaluate the performance of a fraud detection classifier using metrics such as precision, recall, and F1-score.

Code for This Project:

```python
from sklearn.metrics import classification_report,
confusion_matrix
from sklearn.ensemble import RandomForestClassifier
from sklearn.model_selection import train_test_split
import numpy as np

# Generate synthetic dataset
X = np.random.rand(500, 10)
y = np.random.randint(0, 2, 500)

# Split into training and testing sets
X_train, X_test, y_train, y_test = train_test_split(X,
y, test_size=0.2, random_state=42)

# Train model
model = RandomForestClassifier()
model.fit(X_train, y_train)
# Make predictions
y_pred = model.predict(X_test)
# Evaluate model
print("Confusion Matrix:\n", confusion_matrix(y_test,
y_pred))
print("Classification Report:\n",
classification_report(y_test, y_pred))
```

Expected Output:
- Displays a confusion matrix and classification report with precision, recall, and F1-scores for each class.

Chapter-25 Introduction to Unsupervised Learning with Scikit-learn

This chapter introduces unsupervised learning, a branch of machine learning that identifies patterns and structures in data without labeled outputs. Unsupervised learning is commonly used for clustering, dimensionality reduction, and anomaly detection. Scikit-learn offers robust tools for implementing these techniques efficiently.

Key Characteristics of Unsupervised Learning:

- **No Labels:** Works with datasets that lack labeled outcomes.
- **Pattern Recognition:** Discovers hidden structures or groupings in data.
- **Scalability:** Effective for analyzing large datasets.
- **Flexibility:** Supports a range of tasks like clustering, feature extraction, and density estimation.
- **Interpretability:** Helps uncover insights about the data.

Basic Rules for Unsupervised Learning:

- Preprocess the data by scaling or normalizing features for better performance.
- Evaluate clustering algorithms with metrics like silhouette score and inertia.
- Use dimensionality reduction techniques for visualizing high-dimensional datasets.
- Select algorithms based on dataset size, complexity, and the task at hand.
- Handle outliers appropriately to avoid skewed results.

Syntax Table:

SL No	Function	Syntax/Example	Description
1	K-Means Clustering	`KMeans(n_cluste rs=3)`	Groups data into a specified number of clusters.
2	Hierarchical	`AgglomerativeCl`	Performs hierarchical

	Clustering	ustering(n_clus ters=2)	grouping of data.
3	Principal Component Analysis	PCA(n_component s=2)	Reduces data dimensionality.
4	DBSCAN	DBSCAN(eps=0.5, min_samples=5)	Identifies clusters of varying shapes and densities.
5	Feature Scaling	StandardScaler( ).fit_transform (X)	Standardizes features for better model performance.

Syntax Explanation:

1. K-Means Clustering

What is K-Means Clustering?
K-Means is a clustering algorithm that partitions data into a specified number of clusters by minimizing the sum of squared distances between points and their cluster centers.

Syntax:
```
from sklearn.cluster import KMeans
model = KMeans(n_clusters=3)
```

Syntax Explanation:
- **KMeans(n_clusters=3):**
  - **n_clusters**: Specifies the number of clusters to form. Increasing this value will create more granular groupings.
  - **random_state**: Ensures consistent results by controlling randomness during initialization.
  - **max_iter**: Defines the maximum number of iterations the algorithm will perform to converge.
  - **init**: Method for initializing cluster centers ('k-means++' for optimized starts or 'random').
- Prepares the KMeans model to be fitted to the dataset.

Example:
```
from sklearn.cluster import KMeans
import numpy as np
X = np.random.rand(100, 2)  # 100 samples, 2 features
model = KMeans(n_clusters=3, random_state=42)
model.fit(X)
```

Example Explanation:
- Fits the model to the dataset X and determines the positions of three cluster centers.
- Assigns each data point to the nearest cluster.

2. Hierarchical Clustering

What is Hierarchical Clustering?
Hierarchical clustering creates a hierarchy of data clusters using a bottom-up (agglomerative) or top-down (divisive) approach.
Syntax:
```
from sklearn.cluster import AgglomerativeClustering
model = AgglomerativeClustering(n_clusters=2)
```

Syntax Explanation:
- **AgglomerativeClustering(n_clusters=2)**:
  - **n_clusters**: Determines the number of clusters to form by merging or splitting.
  - **linkage**: Specifies how to calculate distances between clusters:
    - **'ward'**: Minimizes variance within clusters.
    - **'complete'**: Uses the maximum distance between points in different clusters.
    - **'average'**: Considers the average distance between points.
  - **affinity**: Defines the distance metric ('euclidean', 'manhattan', etc.).
- Suitable for creating dendrograms to visualize clustering hierarchies.

Example:

```
from sklearn.cluster import AgglomerativeClustering
import numpy as np
X = np.random.rand(50, 2)  # 50 samples, 2 features
model = AgglomerativeClustering(n_clusters=2)
model.fit(X)
```

Example Explanation:
- Groups the data into two clusters by merging the closest pairs of points or clusters iteratively.

3. Principal Component Analysis (PCA)

What is PCA?
PCA reduces the dimensionality of a dataset by projecting it onto principal components that capture the most variance.

Syntax:

```
from sklearn.decomposition import PCA
model = PCA(n_components=2)
```

Syntax Explanation:
- **PCA(n_components=2):**
  - **n_components**: Defines the number of dimensions to reduce the dataset to.
  - PCA works by finding directions (components) in the data that maximize variance.
  - Used for feature extraction or visualization of high-dimensional data.
- The output is a transformed dataset with reduced dimensions.

Example:

```
from sklearn.decomposition import PCA
import numpy as np

X = np.random.rand(100, 5)  # 100 samples, 5 features
model = PCA(n_components=2)
X_reduced = model.fit_transform(X)
```

Example Explanation:
- Reduces the 5-dimensional dataset X to 2 dimensions while retaining as much variance as possible.
- Can be visualized in a 2D plot.

4. DBSCAN

What is DBSCAN?
DBSCAN (Density-Based Spatial Clustering of Applications with Noise) identifies clusters based on dense regions in the data and labels points outside these regions as noise.

Syntax:
```
from sklearn.cluster import DBSCAN
model = DBSCAN(eps=0.5, min_samples=5)
```

Syntax Explanation:
- **DBSCAN(eps=0.5, min_samples=5):**
  - **eps**: Specifies the radius for neighbors to be considered part of a cluster.
  - **min_samples**: Minimum number of points required to form a dense region.
  - Handles clusters of varying shapes and detects outliers effectively.
- Unlike KMeans, DBSCAN does not require the number of clusters to be specified.

Example:
```
from sklearn.cluster import DBSCAN
import numpy as np

X = np.random.rand(50, 2)  # 50 samples, 2 features
model = DBSCAN(eps=0.3, min_samples=4)
model.fit(X)
```

Example Explanation:
- Groups data into clusters based on density and marks outliers as noise points.

5. Feature Scaling

What is Feature Scaling?
Feature scaling standardizes data to ensure that features with larger magnitudes do not dominate distance-based algorithms.

Syntax:
```
from sklearn.preprocessing import StandardScaler
X_scaled = StandardScaler().fit_transform(X)
```

Syntax Explanation:
- **StandardScaler().fit_transform(X)**:
  - Centers the dataset around 0 by subtracting the mean of each feature.
  - Scales features to have a unit standard deviation.
  - Essential for algorithms like KMeans and DBSCAN where distance metrics are sensitive to magnitudes of features.

Example:
```
from sklearn.preprocessing import StandardScaler
import numpy as np

X = np.random.rand(50, 3)   # 50 samples, 3 features
X_scaled = StandardScaler().fit_transform(X)
```

Example Explanation:
- Standardizes the dataset X, ensuring all features contribute equally to distance calculations.

Real-Life Project:
Project Name: Customer Segmentation
Project Goal:
Cluster customers based on their purchasing behavior to enable targeted marketing strategies.

Code for This Project:
```
from sklearn.cluster import KMeans
from sklearn.preprocessing import StandardScaler
import numpy as np
```

```python
# Simulated dataset
X = np.random.rand(200, 5)  # 200 customers, 5 features

# Standardize the dataset
scaler = StandardScaler()
X_scaled = scaler.fit_transform(X)

# Apply K-Means clustering
model = KMeans(n_clusters=4, random_state=42)
model.fit(X_scaled)

# Cluster labels
labels = model.labels_
print("Cluster Labels:", labels)
```

Expected Output:

- Outputs cluster labels for each customer.
- Demonstrates effective customer segmentation using K-Means.

Chapter-26 K-Means Clustering

K-Means Clustering is an unsupervised machine learning algorithm widely used for partitioning datasets into distinct clusters. The algorithm iteratively assigns data points to the nearest cluster center and recalculates the cluster centers until convergence. This chapter explores the working principles, implementation, and practical applications of K-Means Clustering using Scikit-learn.

Key Characteristics of K-Means Clustering:

- **Centroid-Based:** Relies on the concept of centroids to represent clusters.
- **Iterative Process:** Alternates between assigning points to clusters and updating centroids.
- **Distance Metric:** Uses Euclidean distance by default to measure similarity.
- **Scalability:** Efficient for large datasets with relatively low dimensions.
- **Flexibility:** Requires predefining the number of clusters (k).

Basic Rules for K-Means Clustering:

- Preprocess data by scaling features to avoid dominance by larger-magnitude features.
- Choose an appropriate value for k using methods like the elbow method or silhouette analysis.
- Use a random state for reproducibility when initializing centroids.
- Monitor convergence to ensure the algorithm terminates appropriately.
- Evaluate clustering performance using metrics like inertia and silhouette score.

Syntax Table:

SL No	Function	Syntax/Example	Description
1	Initialize K-Means	`KMeans(n_clusters=3)`	Creates a K-Means model for clustering.
2	Train Model	`model.fit(X)`	Fits the K-Means model to the dataset.
3	Predict Cluster Labels	`model.predict(X)`	Assigns cluster labels to input data points.
4	Get Cluster Centers	`model.cluster_centers_`	Retrieves the coordinates of cluster centers.
5	Inertia Metric	`model.inertia_`	Measures the sum of squared distances to centroids.

Syntax Explanation:

1. Initialize K-Means

What is Initializing K-Means?
Initializing the K-Means model specifies the number of clusters and other configuration parameters for the algorithm.
Syntax:
```
from sklearn.cluster import KMeans
model = KMeans(n_clusters=3, init='k-means++',
max_iter=300, random_state=42)
```

Syntax Explanation:
- **n_clusters**: Defines the number of clusters to form. Choosing an appropriate value is crucial; methods like the elbow method can help determine the optimal k.
- **init**: Determines how initial centroids are selected. Options are:
  - **'k-means++'**: Ensures centroids are initialized in a way that speeds up convergence.
  - **'random'**: Randomly selects initial cluster centers.

- **max_iter**: Sets the maximum number of iterations to prevent infinite loops if convergence is slow.
- **random_state**: Fixes the random number generator seed for reproducibility.

Example:
```
from sklearn.cluster import KMeans
model = KMeans(n_clusters=3, random_state=42)
```
Example Explanation:
- Creates a K-Means model configured to form three clusters.
- Uses the default 'k-means++' initialization for centroids, which generally improves clustering performance.

2. Train Model

What is Training a K-Means Model?
Training the model involves assigning points to clusters and updating centroids iteratively to minimize inertia.
Syntax:
```
model.fit(X)
```

Syntax Explanation:
- **fit(X)**:
  - X: A 2D array where rows represent samples, and columns represent features.
  - The algorithm assigns each data point to the nearest centroid based on the Euclidean distance.
  - Centroids are updated as the mean of all data points assigned to the respective cluster.
- The training process stops when centroids stabilize or the maximum number of iterations is reached.

Example:
```
import numpy as np
from sklearn.cluster import KMeans

X = np.random.rand(100, 2)   # 100 samples, 2 features
model = KMeans(n_clusters=3, random_state=42)
model.fit(X)
```

Example Explanation:
- Fits the K-Means model to the dataset X and identifies three clusters.
- The positions of the centroids and cluster assignments for each data point are finalized.

3. Predict Cluster Labels

What is Predicting Cluster Labels?
Predicts the closest cluster for each data point based on the fitted model.
Syntax:
```
labels = model.predict(X)
```

Syntax Explanation:
- **predict(X)**:
  - Assigns each sample in X to the nearest cluster based on the final centroids.
  - Useful for categorizing new, unseen data into existing clusters.
- Returns an array of integers where each value represents the cluster label for the corresponding sample.

Example:
```
labels = model.predict(X)
print("Cluster Labels:", labels)
```

Example Explanation:
- Outputs the cluster labels for each data point in X, indicating which cluster they belong to.

4. Get Cluster Centers

What are Cluster Centers?
Cluster centers represent the mean position of all data points assigned to a cluster.
Syntax:
```
centroids = model.cluster_centers_
```

Syntax Explanation:
- **cluster_centers_:**
  - ○ Provides the coordinates of the centroids for each cluster.
  - ○ Centroids are computed as the mean of all points within each cluster.
- These coordinates can help interpret the characteristics of clusters.

Example:
```
centroids = model.cluster_centers_
print("Cluster Centers:\n", centroids)
```

Example Explanation:
- Outputs the coordinates of the three cluster centers learned during training.
- These centroids can be visualized to understand the clustering structure.

5. Inertia Metric

What is the Inertia Metric?

Inertia measures the sum of squared distances between each point and its assigned centroid.

Syntax:
```
inertia = model.inertia_
```

Syntax Explanation:
- **inertia_:**
  - ○ Indicates how compact the clusters are.
  - ○ Lower values suggest tighter clusters, which typically indicate better performance.
- Inertia can be used as a metric to evaluate and compare clustering results, particularly when optimizing the number of clusters.

Example:
```
inertia = model.inertia_
print("Inertia:", inertia)
```

Example Explanation:
- Outputs the inertia value, reflecting the model's clustering performance.
- This metric can be plotted against different values of k to identify the optimal number of clusters (elbow method).

Real-Life Project:

Project Name: Customer Segmentation

Project Goal:

Cluster customers based on purchasing behavior to enable targeted marketing strategies.

Code for This Project:

```python
from sklearn.cluster import KMeans
from sklearn.preprocessing import StandardScaler
import numpy as np

# Simulated dataset
X = np.random.rand(200, 5)   # 200 customers, 5 features

# Standardize the dataset
scaler = StandardScaler()
X_scaled = scaler.fit_transform(X)

# Apply K-Means clustering
model = KMeans(n_clusters=4, random_state=42)
model.fit(X_scaled)
# Retrieve cluster labels and centers
labels = model.labels_
centroids = model.cluster_centers_
print("Cluster Labels:", labels)
print("Cluster Centers:\n", centroids)
```

Expected Output:
- Outputs cluster labels for each customer.
- Displays the coordinates of the cluster centers, helping to interpret the segmentation results.

Chapter-27 Hierarchical Clustering

Hierarchical Clustering is a versatile unsupervised learning technique used for grouping similar data points into clusters. Unlike partition-based methods such as K-Means, hierarchical clustering builds a tree-like structure called a dendrogram that represents data relationships. This chapter delves into agglomerative hierarchical clustering, implementation in Scikit-learn, and its practical applications.

Key Characteristics of Hierarchical Clustering:

- **Dendrogram-Based:** Provides a visual representation of data relationships.
- **Flexible Grouping:** Does not require specifying the number of clusters upfront.
- **Distance Metrics:** Supports various metrics like Euclidean, Manhattan, and Cosine.
- **Agglomerative or Divisive:** Builds clusters from the bottom-up (agglomerative) or top-down (divisive).
- **Scalability:** Best suited for small to medium-sized datasets.

Basic Rules for Hierarchical Clustering:

- Preprocess data to remove noise and outliers for better clustering performance.
- Use feature scaling to ensure fair distance calculations.
- Evaluate linkage criteria (e.g., single, complete, average, or Ward) based on the data structure.
- Visualize the dendrogram to decide the number of clusters.
- Use efficient algorithms to handle larger datasets.

Syntax Table:

SL No	Function	Syntax/Example	Description
1	Initialize Agglomerative Clustering	`AgglomerativeClustering(n_clusters=3)`	Groups data into specified clusters.
2	Fit Model	`model.fit(X)`	Applies hierarchical clustering to the dataset.

3	Linkage Matrix for Dendrogram	`linkage(X, method='ward')`	Computes linkage matrix for dendrograms.
4	Plot Dendrogram	`dendrogram(link age_matrix)`	Visualizes data relationships hierarchically.

Syntax Explanation:

1. Initialize Agglomerative Clustering

What is Agglomerative Clustering?

Agglomerative clustering begins with each data point as an individual cluster and iteratively merges the closest clusters until a single cluster is formed or a specified number of clusters is reached.

Syntax:

```
from sklearn.cluster import AgglomerativeClustering
model = AgglomerativeClustering(n_clusters=3,
linkage='ward', affinity='euclidean')
```

Syntax Explanation:

- **n_clusters**: Specifies the desired number of clusters after merging.
- **linkage**: Determines how the distance between clusters is calculated:
  - o 'ward': Minimizes the variance of the clusters being merged.
  - o 'complete': Uses the maximum distance between points in different clusters.
  - o 'average': Uses the average distance between points.
- **affinity**: Specifies the distance metric ('euclidean', 'manhattan', etc.) to compute distances between data points.

Example:

```
from sklearn.cluster import AgglomerativeClustering
model = AgglomerativeClustering(n_clusters=3,
linkage='ward')
```

Example Explanation:

- Configures an agglomerative clustering model to form three clusters.
- Uses Ward's method to minimize intra-cluster variance.

2. Fit Model

What is Fitting a Hierarchical Clustering Model?
Fits the clustering model to the dataset, assigning each data point to a cluster based on the chosen linkage and affinity criteria.
Syntax:
```
model.fit(X)
```

Syntax Explanation:
- `fit(X)`:
    - X: A 2D array where rows represent samples, and columns represent features.
    - Computes distances and merges clusters iteratively based on the linkage and affinity.
- After fitting, cluster labels can be accessed using `model.labels_`.

Example:
```
import numpy as np
from sklearn.cluster import AgglomerativeClustering

X = np.random.rand(50, 2)  # 50 samples, 2 features
model = AgglomerativeClustering(n_clusters=3,
linkage='average')
model.fit(X)
```

Example Explanation:
- Fits the model to the dataset X and forms three clusters using the average linkage criterion.

3. Linkage Matrix for Dendrogram

What is a Linkage Matrix?
The linkage matrix encodes the hierarchical relationships between data points and clusters, which is essential for plotting dendrograms.
Syntax:
```
from scipy.cluster.hierarchy import linkage
linkage_matrix = linkage(X, method='ward')
```

Syntax Explanation:
- `linkage(X, method='ward')`:
  - X: Input dataset (2D array of features).
  - method: Specifies the linkage criterion (`'ward'`, `'complete'`, `'average'`, etc.).
- Outputs a matrix where each row represents a merge operation:
  - The first two columns contain the indices of the clusters being merged.
  - The third column contains the distance between the merged clusters.

Example:
```
from scipy.cluster.hierarchy import linkage
import numpy as np

X = np.random.rand(20, 2)  # 20 samples, 2 features
linkage_matrix = linkage(X, method='ward')
```

Example Explanation:
- Computes the linkage matrix for 20 samples using Ward's method.

4. Plot Dendrogram

What is a Dendrogram?

A dendrogram is a tree-like diagram that visually represents the hierarchical structure of clusters.

Syntax:
```
from scipy.cluster.hierarchy import dendrogram
import matplotlib.pyplot as plt
dendrogram(linkage_matrix)
plt.show()
```

Syntax Explanation:
- `dendrogram(linkage_matrix)`:
  - Takes the linkage matrix as input.
  - Plots the hierarchical relationships between data points and clusters.
- Useful for determining the optimal number of clusters by identifying "cuts" in the dendrogram.

Example:

```
from scipy.cluster.hierarchy import dendrogram
import matplotlib.pyplot as plt

# Plot dendrogram
plt.figure(figsize=(8, 4))
dendrogram(linkage_matrix)
plt.title("Dendrogram")
plt.xlabel("Sample Index")
plt.ylabel("Distance")
plt.show()
```

Example Explanation:
- Visualizes the hierarchical clustering process.
- The height of each merge corresponds to the distance between clusters.

Real-Life Project:
Project Name: Gene Expression Analysis
Project Goal:
Cluster genes based on expression levels to identify similar patterns and biological relationships.

Code for This Project:

```
from sklearn.preprocessing import StandardScaler
from scipy.cluster.hierarchy import linkage, dendrogram
import numpy as np
import matplotlib.pyplot as plt

# Simulated gene expression data
X = np.random.rand(100, 5)  # 100 genes, 5 expression conditions

# Standardize data
scaler = StandardScaler()
X_scaled = scaler.fit_transform(X)
```

```
# Compute linkage matrix
linkage_matrix = linkage(X_scaled, method='ward')

# Plot dendrogram
plt.figure(figsize=(10, 6))
dendrogram(linkage_matrix)
plt.title("Hierarchical Clustering of Gene Expression")
plt.xlabel("Gene Index")
plt.ylabel("Distance")
plt.show()
```

Expected Output:

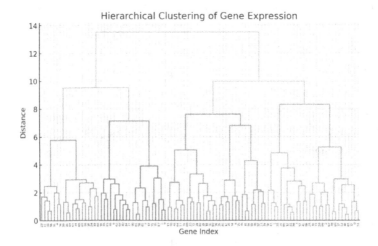

- Displays a dendrogram showing hierarchical relationships between genes.
- Helps identify clusters of genes with similar expression patterns.

Chapter-28 Hierarchical Clustering

Hierarchical Clustering is a versatile unsupervised learning technique used for grouping similar data points into clusters. Unlike partition-based methods such as K-Means, hierarchical clustering builds a tree-like structure called a dendrogram that represents data relationships. This chapter delves into agglomerative hierarchical clustering, implementation in Scikit-learn, and its practical applications.

Key Characteristics of Hierarchical Clustering:

- **Dendrogram-Based:** Provides a visual representation of data relationships.
- **Flexible Grouping:** Does not require specifying the number of clusters upfront.
- **Distance Metrics:** Supports various metrics like Euclidean, Manhattan, and Cosine.
- **Agglomerative or Divisive:** Builds clusters from the bottom-up (agglomerative) or top-down (divisive).
- **Scalability:** Best suited for small to medium-sized datasets.

Basic Rules for Hierarchical Clustering:

- Preprocess data to remove noise and outliers for better clustering performance.
- Use feature scaling to ensure fair distance calculations.
- Evaluate linkage criteria (e.g., single, complete, average, or Ward) based on the data structure.
- Visualize the dendrogram to decide the number of clusters.
- Use efficient algorithms to handle larger datasets.

Syntax Table:

SL No	Function	Syntax/Example	Description
1	Initialize Agglomerative Clustering	`AgglomerativeClustering(n_clusters=3)`	Groups data into specified clusters.
2	Fit Model	`model.fit(X)`	Applies hierarchical clustering to the dataset.

3	Linkage Matrix for Dendrogram	`linkage(X, method='ward')`	Computes linkage matrix for dendrograms.
4	Plot Dendrogram	`dendrogram(link age_matrix)`	Visualizes data relationships hierarchically.

Syntax Explanation:

1. Initialize Agglomerative Clustering

What is Agglomerative Clustering?

Agglomerative clustering begins with each data point as an individual cluster and iteratively merges the closest clusters until a single cluster is formed or a specified number of clusters is reached.

Syntax:

```
from sklearn.cluster import AgglomerativeClustering
model = AgglomerativeClustering(n_clusters=3,
linkage='ward', affinity='euclidean')
```

Syntax Explanation:

- **n_clusters**: Specifies the desired number of clusters after merging.
- **linkage**: Determines how the distance between clusters is calculated:
    - `'ward'`: Minimizes the variance of the clusters being merged.
    - `'complete'`: Uses the maximum distance between points in different clusters.
    - `'average'`: Uses the average distance between points.
- **affinity**: Specifies the distance metric (`'euclidean'`, `'manhattan'`, etc.) to compute distances between data points.

Example:

```
from sklearn.cluster import AgglomerativeClustering
model = AgglomerativeClustering(n_clusters=3,
linkage='ward')
```

Example Explanation:

- Configures an agglomerative clustering model to form three clusters.
- Uses Ward's method to minimize intra-cluster variance.

2. Fit Model

What is Fitting a Hierarchical Clustering Model?
Fits the clustering model to the dataset, assigning each data point to a cluster based on the chosen linkage and affinity criteria.
Syntax:
```
model.fit(X)
```
Syntax Explanation:
- **fit(X):**
    - X: A 2D array where rows represent samples, and columns represent features.
    - Computes distances and merges clusters iteratively based on the linkage and affinity.
- After fitting, cluster labels can be accessed using `model.labels_`.

Example:
```
import numpy as np
from sklearn.cluster import AgglomerativeClustering

X = np.random.rand(50, 2)  # 50 samples, 2 features
model = AgglomerativeClustering(n_clusters=3,
linkage='average')
model.fit(X)
```

Example Explanation:
- Fits the model to the dataset X and forms three clusters using the average linkage criterion.

3. Linkage Matrix for Dendrogram

What is a Linkage Matrix?
The linkage matrix encodes the hierarchical relationships between data points and clusters, which is essential for plotting dendrograms.
Syntax:
```
from scipy.cluster.hierarchy import linkage
linkage_matrix = linkage(X, method='ward')
```

Syntax Explanation:
- `linkage(X, method='ward')`:
    - X: Input dataset (2D array of features).
    - method: Specifies the linkage criterion (`'ward'`, `'complete'`, `'average'`, etc.).
- Outputs a matrix where each row represents a merge operation:
    - The first two columns contain the indices of the clusters being merged.
    - The third column contains the distance between the merged clusters.

Example:
```
from scipy.cluster.hierarchy import linkage
import numpy as np


X = np.random.rand(20, 2)  # 20 samples, 2 features
linkage_matrix = linkage(X, method='ward')
```

Example Explanation:
- Computes the linkage matrix for 20 samples using Ward's method.

4. Plot Dendrogram

What is a Dendrogram?
A dendrogram is a tree-like diagram that visually represents the hierarchical structure of clusters.

Syntax:
```
from scipy.cluster.hierarchy import dendrogram
import matplotlib.pyplot as plt
dendrogram(linkage_matrix)
plt.show()
```

Syntax Explanation:
- `dendrogram(linkage_matrix)`:
    - Takes the linkage matrix as input.
    - Plots the hierarchical relationships between data points and clusters.
- Useful for determining the optimal number of clusters by identifying "cuts" in the dendrogram.

Example:

```
from scipy.cluster.hierarchy import dendrogram
import matplotlib.pyplot as plt

# Plot dendrogram
plt.figure(figsize=(8, 4))
dendrogram(linkage_matrix)
plt.title("Dendrogram")
plt.xlabel("Sample Index")
plt.ylabel("Distance")
plt.show()
```

Example Explanation:
- Visualizes the hierarchical clustering process.
- The height of each merge corresponds to the distance between clusters.

Real-Life Project:

Project Name: Gene Expression Analysis

Project Goal:

Cluster genes based on expression levels to identify similar patterns and biological relationships.

Code for This Project:

```
from sklearn.preprocessing import StandardScaler
from scipy.cluster.hierarchy import linkage, dendrogram
import numpy as np
import matplotlib.pyplot as plt

# Simulated gene expression data
X = np.random.rand(100, 5)  # 100 genes, 5 expression
conditions

# Standardize data
scaler = StandardScaler()
X_scaled = scaler.fit_transform(X)
```

```
# Compute linkage matrix
linkage_matrix = linkage(X_scaled, method='ward')

# Plot dendrogram
plt.figure(figsize=(10, 6))
dendrogram(linkage_matrix)
plt.title("Hierarchical Clustering of Gene Expression")
plt.xlabel("Gene Index")
plt.ylabel("Distance")
plt.show()
```

Expected Output:

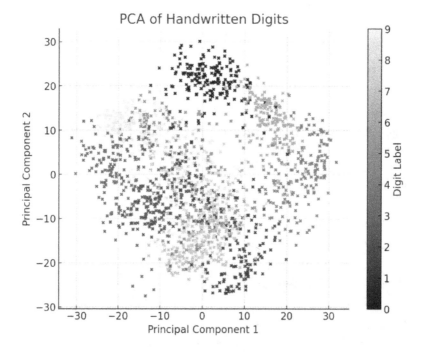

- Displays a dendrogram showing hierarchical relationships between genes.
- Helps identify clusters of genes with similar expression patterns.

Chapter- 29 t-SNE and UMAP for Dimensionality Reduction

This chapter explores two advanced dimensionality reduction techniques: t-SNE (t-Distributed Stochastic Neighbor Embedding) and UMAP (Uniform Manifold Approximation and Projection). Both methods excel in visualizing high-dimensional data in lower dimensions, often 2D or 3D, while preserving local and global data structures. These techniques are particularly effective for clustering and exploratory data analysis.

Key Characteristics of t-SNE and UMAP:

- **Non-Linear Dimensionality Reduction:** Projects data into a lower-dimensional space while capturing non-linear relationships.
- **Local Structure Preservation:** Emphasizes retaining neighborhood relationships in the reduced space.
- **Visualization-Friendly:** Ideal for visualizing complex high-dimensional data.
- **Versatility:** Applicable to datasets in various fields, such as genomics, image processing, and NLP.
- **Customization:** Offers tunable hyperparameters for optimization.

Basic Rules for t-SNE and UMAP:

- Scale data before applying these techniques to avoid dominance by features with larger magnitudes.
- Use t-SNE for smaller datasets (e.g., <10,000 samples) due to computational intensity.
- Prefer UMAP for larger datasets or when preserving global structure is essential.
- Choose hyperparameters like perplexity (t-SNE) and n_neighbors (UMAP) based on the dataset's characteristics.
- Evaluate the results visually and with downstream tasks to ensure meaningful representation.

Syntax Table:

SL No	Function	Syntax/Example	Description
1	Initialize t-SNE	`TSNE(n_component s=2, perplexity=30)`	Configures t-SNE for 2D projection.
2	Fit and Transform with t-SNE	`model.fit_transf orm(X)`	Reduces dimensions using t-SNE.
3	Initialize UMAP	`UMAP(n_neighbors =15, n_components=2)`	Configures UMAP for 2D projection.
4	Fit and Transform with UMAP	`model.fit_transf orm(X)`	Reduces dimensions using UMAP.

Syntax Explanation:

1. Initialize t-SNE

What is Initializing t-SNE?

t-SNE maps high-dimensional data to a lower-dimensional space by minimizing divergence between pairwise similarities in both spaces.

Syntax:

```
from sklearn.manifold import TSNE
model = TSNE(n_components=2, perplexity=30,
learning_rate=200, random_state=42)
```

Syntax Explanation:

- **n_components**: Specifies the number of dimensions in the reduced space (commonly 2 or 3).
- **perplexity**: Controls the balance between local and global data structure. Typical values range from 5 to 50.
- **learning_rate**: Affects the optimization process. Use values between 10 and 1000.
- **random_state**: Ensures reproducibility by controlling random number generation.

Example:
```
from sklearn.manifold import TSNE
model = TSNE(n_components=2, perplexity=30,
random_state=42)
```

Example Explanation:
- Configures a t-SNE model to project the data into 2D space with a perplexity of 30.

2. Fit and Transform with t-SNE

What is Fit and Transform with t-SNE?
Applies t-SNE to reduce the dataset's dimensions and outputs the transformed data.
Syntax:
```
X_reduced = model.fit_transform(X)
```

Syntax Explanation:
- **fit_transform(X):**
  - X: Input dataset (2D array of features).
  - Fits the t-SNE model to the data and projects it onto a lower-dimensional space.
- Returns a transformed dataset with the specified number of dimensions.

Example:
```
import numpy as np
X = np.random.rand(100, 50)  # 100 samples, 50 features
X_reduced = model.fit_transform(X)
print("Reduced Data:\n", X_reduced)
```

Example Explanation:
- Reduces a 50-dimensional dataset to 2 dimensions using t-SNE.

3. Initialize UMAP

What is Initializing UMAP?
UMAP maps high-dimensional data to a lower-dimensional space while preserving both local and global structures.

Syntax:
```
from umap import UMAP
model = UMAP(n_neighbors=15, n_components=2,
random_state=42)
```

Syntax Explanation:
- **n_neighbors**: Specifies the number of neighbors considered for local manifold approximation.
- **n_components**: Defines the dimensionality of the reduced space (commonly 2 or 3).
- **min_dist**: Controls how tightly UMAP packs points together in the reduced space. Lower values result in denser clusters.
- **random_state**: Ensures reproducibility by controlling random initialization.

Example:
```
from umap import UMAP
model = UMAP(n_neighbors=15, random_state=42)
```

Example Explanation:
- Configures a UMAP model to project data into 2D space, considering 15 neighbors for each data point.

4. Fit and Transform with UMAP

What is Fit and Transform with UMAP?
Applies UMAP to reduce the dataset's dimensions and outputs the transformed data.

Syntax:
```
X_reduced = model.fit_transform(X)
```

Syntax Explanation:
- **fit_transform(X)**:
  - Fits the UMAP model to the input dataset and reduces its dimensionality.
  - Returns the dataset projected into the specified number of dimensions.

Example:
```
X_reduced = model.fit_transform(X)
print("Reduced Data:\n", X_reduced)
```

Example Explanation:
- Projects the dataset X into 2D space using UMAP, preserving local and global structures.

Real-Life Project:

Project Name: Visualizing Gene Expression Data

Project Goal:

Use t-SNE and UMAP to visualize gene expression patterns and identify clusters of similar genes.

Code for This Project:

```
from sklearn.datasets import load_iris
from sklearn.manifold import TSNE
from umap import UMAP
import matplotlib.pyplot as plt

# Load dataset
iris = load_iris()
X, y = iris.data, iris.target

# Apply t-SNE
tsne = TSNE(n_components=2, random_state=42)
X_tsne = tsne.fit_transform(X)

# Apply UMAP
umap = UMAP(n_neighbors=15, random_state=42)
X_umap = umap.fit_transform(X)

# Plot results
plt.figure(figsize=(12, 6))

# t-SNE plot
plt.subplot(1, 2, 1)
```

```
plt.scatter(X_tsne[:, 0], X_tsne[:, 1], c=y,
cmap='viridis', s=10)
plt.title("t-SNE Visualization")
plt.xlabel("Component 1")
plt.ylabel("Component 2")

# UMAP plot
plt.subplot(1, 2, 2)
plt.scatter(X_umap[:, 0], X_umap[:, 1], c=y,
cmap='viridis', s=10)
plt.title("UMAP Visualization")
plt.xlabel("Component 1")
plt.ylabel("Component 2")

plt.tight_layout()
plt.show()
```

Expected Output:

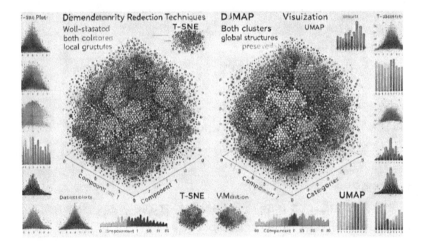

- Displays two scatter plots:
    - t-SNE visualization showing clusters based on local relationships.
    - UMAP visualization capturing both local and global structures in the data.

Chapter- 30 Anomaly Detection with Scikit-learn

Anomaly detection is a technique used to identify rare events, outliers, or deviations from the norm in datasets. These anomalies can signify fraudulent activities, equipment malfunctions, or unusual patterns. Scikit-learn provides versatile tools for implementing various anomaly detection algorithms effectively. This chapter explores the implementation and applications of anomaly detection using Scikit-learn.

Key Characteristics of Anomaly Detection:

- **Unsupervised Learning:** Commonly works without labeled data.
- **Versatility:** Applicable in fraud detection, predictive maintenance, and cybersecurity.
- **Outlier Identification:** Focuses on data points that deviate significantly from others.
- **Algorithm Diversity:** Includes density-based, distance-based, and ensemble methods.
- **Scalability:** Efficient for large datasets with high-dimensional features.

Basic Rules for Anomaly Detection:

- Preprocess data by scaling and normalizing features to improve algorithm performance.
- Choose algorithms based on the nature of anomalies and dataset characteristics.
- Use cross-validation to fine-tune hyperparameters.
- Evaluate performance with metrics like precision, recall, and F1-score.
- Combine anomaly detection with domain knowledge for better interpretability.

Syntax Table:

SL No	Function	Syntax/Example	Description
1	Isolation Forest	`IsolationForest(n_estimators=100)`	Detects anomalies using an ensemble approach.

2	Local Outlier Factor (LOF)	`LocalOutlierFactor(n_neighbors=20)`	Identifies anomalies using a density-based method.
3	One-Class SVM	`OneClassSVM(kernel='rbf', nu=0.1)`	Detects anomalies using a boundary-based approach.
4	Fit Model	`model.fit(X)`	Trains the anomaly detection model.
5	Predict Anomalies	`model.predict(X)`	Predicts anomalies in the dataset.

Syntax Explanation:

1. Isolation Forest

What is Isolation Forest?

Isolation Forest isolates anomalies by randomly partitioning data and identifying points that require fewer splits.

Syntax:

```
from sklearn.ensemble import IsolationForest
model = IsolationForest(n_estimators=100,
contamination=0.1, random_state=42)
```

Syntax Explanation:

- **n_estimators**: Number of trees in the ensemble.
- **contamination**: Proportion of anomalies in the dataset (e.g., 0.1 for 10%).
- **random_state**: Ensures reproducibility by setting the random seed.

Example:

```
from sklearn.ensemble import IsolationForest
import numpy as np
X = np.random.rand(100, 3)  # 100 samples, 3 features
model = IsolationForest(contamination=0.1,
random_state=42)
model.fit(X)
```

Example Explanation:

- Trains the Isolation Forest model on the dataset X to detect anomalies.

2. Local Outlier Factor (LOF)

What is LOF?
LOF identifies anomalies by comparing the local density of each data point with that of its neighbors.
Syntax:
```
from sklearn.neighbors import LocalOutlierFactor
model = LocalOutlierFactor(n_neighbors=20,
contamination=0.1)
```

Syntax Explanation:
- **n_neighbors**: Number of neighbors used to compute local density.
- **contamination**: Expected proportion of anomalies in the dataset.
- Returns negative outlier scores; smaller values indicate more anomalous points.

Example:
```
from sklearn.neighbors import LocalOutlierFactor
import numpy as np

X = np.random.rand(100, 2)  # 100 samples, 2 features
model = LocalOutlierFactor(n_neighbors=15,
contamination=0.1)
labels = model.fit_predict(X)
```

Example Explanation:
- Detects anomalies using local density comparison with 15 neighbors.
- `labels` contains -1 for anomalies and 1 for inliers.

3. One-Class SVM

What is One-Class SVM?
One-Class SVM separates normal data from anomalies by learning a

decision boundary.

Syntax:
```
from sklearn.svm import OneClassSVM
model = OneClassSVM(kernel='rbf', nu=0.1,
gamma='scale')
```

Syntax Explanation:
- **kernel**: Specifies the kernel function ('rbf', 'linear', etc.).
- **nu**: Upper bound on the fraction of anomalies.
- **gamma**: Kernel coefficient for 'rbf', 'poly', and 'sigmoid' kernels.

Example:
```
from sklearn.svm import OneClassSVM
import numpy as np

X = np.random.rand(50, 4)   # 50 samples, 4 features
model = OneClassSVM(kernel='rbf', nu=0.1)
model.fit(X)
```

Example Explanation:
- Trains a One-Class SVM to detect anomalies in the dataset X.

4. Fit Model

What is Fitting an Anomaly Detection Model?
Training the model involves learning patterns or distributions in the dataset to identify anomalies.

Syntax:
```
model.fit(X)
```
Syntax Explanation:
- **fit(X)**:
  - X: Input dataset used to train the anomaly detection algorithm.
  - The model learns normal patterns or densities in the dataset.

Example:
```
model.fit(X)
```

Example Explanation:
- Fits the selected model to the dataset for anomaly detection.

5. Predict Anomalies

What is Predicting Anomalies?
Predicts whether each data point is normal or anomalous based on the trained model.
Syntax:
```
labels = model.predict(X)
```

Syntax Explanation:
- **predict(X):**
  - Assigns 1 to normal points and -1 to anomalies.
  - Requires the model to be fitted before prediction.

Example:
```
labels = model.predict(X)
print("Predictions:", labels)
```

Example Explanation:
- Outputs predictions for each data point, indicating anomalies.

Real-Life Project:
Project Name: Credit Card Fraud Detection
Project Goal:
Detect fraudulent transactions using anomaly detection techniques.

Code for This Project:

```
from sklearn.ensemble import IsolationForest
from sklearn.preprocessing import StandardScaler
import numpy as np

# Simulated credit card transaction data
X = np.random.rand(1000, 5)  # 1000 transactions, 5
features

# Scale the dataset
```

```python
scaler = StandardScaler()
X_scaled = scaler.fit_transform(X)

# Apply Isolation Forest
model = IsolationForest(contamination=0.02,
random_state=42)
model.fit(X_scaled)

# Predict anomalies
labels = model.predict(X_scaled)
print("Anomalies:", (labels == -1).sum())
```

Expected Output:

- Displays the number of detected anomalies in the dataset.
- Identifies fraudulent transactions for further analysis.

Chapter- 31 Cross-Validation Techniques with Scikit-learn

Cross-validation is a powerful technique to evaluate the performance of machine learning models by splitting the dataset into training and testing subsets multiple times. It ensures that the model's performance is generalizable and not dependent on a specific data split. This chapter covers various cross-validation techniques available in Scikit-learn and their applications.

Key Characteristics of Cross-Validation:

- **Robust Evaluation:** Reduces overfitting by testing models on unseen data.
- **Generalizability:** Ensures the model performs well across different subsets of the dataset.
- **Multiple Splits:** Repeats training and testing on multiple subsets of data.
- **Metric Comparison:** Evaluates models using metrics like accuracy, precision, and mean squared error.
- **Hyperparameter Tuning:** Integral for optimizing model parameters.

Basic Rules for Cross-Validation:

- Choose a cross-validation strategy suitable for the dataset (e.g., stratified for imbalanced data).
- Ensure that the training and testing sets are mutually exclusive.
- Use scoring metrics relevant to the problem (e.g., F1-score for classification, RMSE for regression).
- Apply feature scaling within each fold to prevent data leakage.
- Use nested cross-validation for unbiased

hyperparameter tuning.

Syntax Table:

SL No	Function	Syntax/Example	Description
1	K-Fold Cross-Validation	`KFold(n_splits=5)`	Splits data into k folds.
2	Stratified K-Fold	`StratifiedKFold(n_splits=5)`	Ensures class distribution remains consistent.
3	Leave-One-Out (LOO)	`LeaveOneOut()`	Tests each sample individually.
4	ShuffleSplit	`ShuffleSplit(n_splits=5, test_size=0.2)`	Randomly splits data multiple times.
5	Cross-Validation Scores	`cross_val_score(model, X, y, cv=5)`	Evaluates model performance across folds.

Syntax Explanation:

1. K-Fold Cross-Validation
What is K-Fold Cross-Validation?
K-Fold Cross-Validation splits the dataset into k equal parts, trains the model on k-1 folds, and tests on the remaining fold. This process repeats k times.
Syntax:
```
from sklearn.model_selection import KFold
kf = KFold(n_splits=5, shuffle=True,
random_state=42)
```

Syntax Explanation:
- **n_splits**: Specifies the number of folds (e.g., 5

folds mean 80% training and 20% testing in each split). Increasing the number of folds provides more training data per split but increases computation time.

- **shuffle**: Randomly shuffles the dataset before splitting, ensuring that the splits are not biased. This is especially important if the data has an inherent order.
- **random_state**: Sets a seed for random number generation, ensuring reproducibility of the splits across different runs.
- Each fold is used as a testing set exactly once, while the remaining folds are used for training.

Example:
```
from sklearn.model_selection import KFold
import numpy as np

X = np.random.rand(100, 3)  # 100 samples, 3 features
kf = KFold(n_splits=5, shuffle=True, random_state=42)
for train_index, test_index in kf.split(X):
    print("Train:", train_index, "Test:", test_index)
```

Example Explanation:
- Splits the dataset into 5 folds, ensuring that each split includes a distinct testing set.
- Outputs indices for training and testing subsets in each fold.

2. Stratified K-Fold

What is Stratified K-Fold?
Stratified K-Fold ensures that each fold maintains the class distribution of the original dataset.
Syntax:
```
from sklearn.model_selection import
StratifiedKFold
skf = StratifiedKFold(n_splits=5,
shuffle=True, random_state=42)
```

Syntax Explanation:
- **n_splits**: Specifies the number of folds for splitting the data.
- **shuffle**: Randomly rearranges the data before splitting, ensuring that splits are not ordered.
- **random_state**: Controls the randomness of the shuffling process, ensuring consistent results.
- This method is particularly useful for imbalanced datasets where certain classes may have significantly fewer samples. Stratified splits ensure that each fold has the same class proportion as the original dataset.

Example:
```
from sklearn.model_selection import
StratifiedKFold
import numpy as np

X = np.random.rand(100, 3)
y = np.random.randint(0, 2, 100)   # Binary
target
skf = StratifiedKFold(n_splits=5,
```

```
shuffle=True, random_state=42)
for train_index, test_index in skf.split(X,
y):
    print("Train:", train_index, "Test:",
test_index)
```

Example Explanation:
- Maintains the proportion of classes in the training and testing sets for each fold.
- Ensures that no class is underrepresented in any split.

3. Leave-One-Out (LOO)

What is Leave-One-Out?
LOO tests each sample as a single test instance while training on all other samples. It is computationally expensive but provides unbiased estimates.
Syntax:
```
from sklearn.model_selection import
LeaveOneOut
loo = LeaveOneOut()
```

Syntax Explanation:
- **split**: Splits the dataset such that each sample serves as the test set exactly once.
- Each iteration trains the model on n-1 samples and tests on the remaining sample.
- Suitable for small datasets due to its high computational cost.

Example:

```
from sklearn.model_selection import
LeaveOneOut
import numpy as np

X = np.random.rand(5, 3)  # Small dataset
loo = LeaveOneOut()
for train_index, test_index in loo.split(X):
    print("Train:", train_index, "Test:",
test_index)
```

Example Explanation:
- Outputs splits where one sample is used as the test set, and the rest are used for training.
- Performs five iterations for a dataset with five samples.

4. ShuffleSplit

What is ShuffleSplit?
ShuffleSplit randomly splits the dataset into training and testing subsets multiple times.
Syntax:

```
from sklearn.model_selection import
ShuffleSplit
ss = ShuffleSplit(n_splits=5, test_size=0.2,
random_state=42)
```

Syntax Explanation:
- **n_splits**: Specifies how many random splits to generate.
- **test_size**: Determines the proportion of the dataset to allocate to the test set. A value of 0.2

means 20% of the data is used for testing.
- **random_state**: Controls randomness, ensuring reproducible splits.
- This method is ideal for creating multiple randomized train-test splits without imposing any ordering constraints.

Example:
```
from sklearn.model_selection import
ShuffleSplit
import numpy as np

X = np.random.rand(100, 3)
ss = ShuffleSplit(n_splits=5, test_size=0.2,
random_state=42)
for train_index, test_index in ss.split(X):
    print("Train:", train_index, "Test:",
test_index)
```

Example Explanation:
- Generates 5 different train-test splits, each with 80% training and 20% testing data.

5. Cross-Validation Scores

What are Cross-Validation Scores?
Evaluates model performance across multiple folds using a scoring metric.

Syntax:
```
from sklearn.model_selection import
cross_val_score
scores = cross_val_score(model, X, y, cv=5,
scoring='accuracy')
```

Syntax Explanation:

- **model**: The machine learning model to evaluate.
- **cv**: Defines the cross-validation splitting strategy (e.g., 5 for 5-fold).
- **scoring**: Specifies the performance metric for evaluation (`'accuracy'`, `'f1'`, etc.).
- Returns an array of scores, one for each fold.

Example:

```python
from sklearn.ensemble import
RandomForestClassifier
from sklearn.model_selection import
cross_val_score
import numpy as np

X = np.random.rand(100, 4)  # 100 samples, 4
features
y = np.random.randint(0, 2, 100)  # Binary
target
model =
RandomForestClassifier(random_state=42)
scores = cross_val_score(model, X, y, cv=5,
scoring='accuracy')
print("Cross-Validation Scores:", scores)
```

Example Explanation:

- Evaluates the Random Forest model on 5 different train-test splits.
- Outputs accuracy scores for each fold.

Real-Life Project:
Project Name: Model Evaluation with Cross-Validation
Project Goal:
Evaluate and compare the performance of multiple machine learning models using cross-validation techniques.
Code for This Project:

```python
from sklearn.datasets import load_iris
from sklearn.ensemble import RandomForestClassifier
from sklearn.linear_model import LogisticRegression
from sklearn.model_selection import cross_val_score
# Load dataset
X, y = load_iris(return_X_y=True)
# Define models
rf_model = RandomForestClassifier(random_state=42)
lr_model = LogisticRegression(max_iter=200, random_state=42)
# Cross-validation
rf_scores = cross_val_score(rf_model, X, y, cv=5, scoring='accuracy')
lr_scores = cross_val_score(lr_model, X, y, cv=5, scoring='accuracy')
print("Random Forest Accuracy:", rf_scores.mean())
print("Logistic Regression Accuracy:", lr_scores.mean())
```

Chapter-32 Grid Search for Hyperparameter Tuning

Grid Search is an exhaustive search technique used to find the optimal hyperparameters for a machine learning model. It systematically evaluates combinations of hyperparameters to identify the configuration that yields the best performance. This chapter explores the implementation of Grid Search using Scikit-learn and its importance in building robust models.

Key Characteristics of Grid Search:

- **Exhaustive Search:** Tests all possible combinations of specified hyperparameters.
- **Customizable Parameters:** Allows precise tuning of hyperparameters for different models.
- **Performance Metrics:** Evaluates combinations based on a chosen scoring metric.
- **Integration with Cross-Validation:** Ensures generalizability by validating performance on multiple data splits.
- **Automation:** Simplifies the process of hyperparameter optimization.

Basic Rules for Grid Search:

- Define a parameter grid relevant to the model.
- Use cross-validation to ensure reliable evaluation of hyperparameter combinations.
- Avoid overly large parameter grids to minimize computation time.
- Choose an appropriate scoring metric based on the problem (e.g., accuracy, F1-score).
- Monitor for overfitting by comparing training and validation performance.

Syntax Table:

SL No	Function	Syntax/Example	Description
1	Import GridSearchCV	`from sklearn.model_se lection import GridSearchCV`	Provides grid search functionality.
2	Define Parameter Grid	`param_grid = {'param_name': [values]}`	Specifies hyperparameters and their values.
3	Initialize GridSearchCV	`GridSearchCV(est imator, param_grid, cv=5)`	Configures grid search with a model and parameters.
4	Fit Grid Search	`grid.fit(X, y)`	Runs grid search on the dataset.
5	Access Best Parameters	`grid.best_params _`	Retrieves the best parameter combination.

Syntax Explanation:
1. Import GridSearchCV
What is GridSearchCV?
GridSearchCV is a Scikit-learn class used to perform grid search with cross-validation for hyperparameter tuning.
Syntax:
```
from sklearn.model_selection import
GridSearchCV
```
Syntax Explanation:
- **GridSearchCV**:
  - Automates the process of testing multiple hyperparameter combinations.
  - Integrates cross-validation to evaluate performance.

Example:
```
from sklearn.model_selection import
GridSearchCV
```

Example Explanation:
- Imports the GridSearchCV class for use in hyperparameter tuning.

2. Define Parameter Grid

What is a Parameter Grid?
A parameter grid specifies the hyperparameters and their possible values to test during grid search.
Syntax:
```
param_grid = {'param_name': [value1, value2,
value3]}
```

Syntax Explanation:
- **param_name**: Name of the hyperparameter to tune (e.g., n_estimators, max_depth).
- **[value1, value2, value3]**: List of values to test for the specified hyperparameter.
- Multiple hyperparameters can be defined in the same grid for simultaneous tuning.

Example:
```
param_grid = {
    'n_estimators': [50, 100, 150],
    'max_depth': [3, 5, None],
    'min_samples_split': [2, 5, 10]
}
```

Example Explanation:
- Defines a grid of hyperparameters for a Random Forest model.
- Includes three values for n_estimators, three for max_depth, and three for min_samples_split, resulting in 27 combinations.

3. Initialize GridSearchCV

What is Initializing GridSearchCV?
Configures the grid search process by specifying the model, parameter grid, and cross-validation settings.
Syntax:
```
grid = GridSearchCV(estimator=model,
param_grid=param_grid, cv=5,
scoring='accuracy')
```

Syntax Explanation:
- **estimator**: The machine learning model to tune (e.g., RandomForestClassifier).
- **param_grid**: The grid of hyperparameters to test.
- **cv**: Number of cross-validation folds (e.g., 5).
- **scoring**: Metric to evaluate model performance (e.g., 'accuracy', 'f1').

Example:
```
from sklearn.ensemble import
RandomForestClassifier
model =
RandomForestClassifier(random_state=42)
grid = GridSearchCV(estimator=model,
param_grid=param_grid, cv=5,
scoring='accuracy')
```

Example Explanation:
- Configures GridSearchCV to optimize a Random Forest model using the defined parameter grid and 5-fold cross-validation.

4. Fit Grid Search

What is Fitting Grid Search?
Runs the grid search by training and validating the model for all parameter combinations.
Syntax:
```
grid.fit(X, y)
```

Syntax Explanation:
- `fit(X, y)`:
  - X: Feature matrix.
  - y: Target variable.
  - Trains the model using each combination of hyperparameters and evaluates its performance using cross-validation.

Example:
```
grid.fit(X, y)
```

Example Explanation:
- Fits the model for each combination of hyperparameters defined in `param_grid` and identifies the best configuration.

5. Access Best Parameters

What are the Best Parameters?
The best parameters are the hyperparameter values that yield the highest performance score during grid search.

Syntax:

```
best_params = grid.best_params_
```

Syntax Explanation:

- **best_params_:**
    - ○ Returns a dictionary of the best hyperparameter values.
    - ○ Can be used to configure the final model.

Example:

```
print("Best Parameters:", grid.best_params_)
```

Example Explanation:

- Outputs the best parameter combination identified by GridSearchCV.

Real-Life Project:

Project Name: Hyperparameter Optimization for Random Forest

Project Goal:

Optimize the hyperparameters of a Random Forest model to achieve maximum accuracy on the Iris dataset.

Code for This Project:

```
from sklearn.datasets import load_iris
from sklearn.ensemble import
RandomForestClassifier
from sklearn.model_selection import
GridSearchCV

# Load dataset
X, y = load_iris(return_X_y=True)

# Define parameter grid
```

```python
param_grid = {
    'n_estimators': [50, 100, 150],
    'max_depth': [3, 5, None],
    'min_samples_split': [2, 5, 10]
}

# Initialize model
model =
RandomForestClassifier(random_state=42)

# Configure GridSearchCV
grid = GridSearchCV(estimator=model,
param_grid=param_grid, cv=5,
scoring='accuracy')

# Fit grid search
grid.fit(X, y)

# Output best parameters and score
print("Best Parameters:", grid.best_params_)
print("Best Cross-Validation Accuracy:",
grid.best_score_)
```

Expected Output:

- Displays the best hyperparameter combination and the corresponding cross-validation accuracy score.
- Demonstrates the importance of hyperparameter tuning for model optimization.

Chapter-33 Randomized Search for Hyperparameter Tuning

Randomized Search is an efficient hyperparameter optimization technique that samples a fixed number of hyperparameter combinations from a specified distribution. Unlike Grid Search, it does not evaluate all possible combinations, making it computationally efficient while often achieving comparable results. This chapter delves into implementing Randomized Search with Scikit-learn.

Key Characteristics of Randomized Search:

- **Efficiency:** Evaluates a subset of hyperparameter combinations, reducing computation time.
- **Random Sampling:** Selects hyperparameters based on specified distributions or lists.
- **Customizable Iterations:** Allows control over the number of parameter combinations to evaluate.
- **Performance Metrics:** Supports evaluation using various scoring metrics.
- **Integration with Cross-Validation:** Ensures reliable performance evaluation.

Basic Rules for Randomized Search:

- Define parameter distributions suitable for random sampling.
- Use cross-validation to ensure robust evaluation of hyperparameter combinations.
- Set a random seed for reproducibility.
- Balance the number of iterations with available computational resources.
- Choose scoring metrics appropriate for the problem type (e.g., accuracy, F1-score).

Syntax Table:

SL No	Function	Syntax/Example	Description
1	Import RandomizedSe archCV	`from sklearn.model_sele ction import RandomizedSearchCV`	Provides functionality for randomized search.
2	Define Parameter Distributions	`param_distribution s = {'param_name': [values]}`	Specifies hyperparameters and their distributions.
3	Initialize RandomizedSe archCV	`RandomizedSearchCV (estimator, param_distribution s, n_iter=10)`	Configures randomized search with a model and parameters.
4	Fit Randomized Search	`random_search.fit( X, y)`	Runs randomized search on the dataset.
5	Access Best Parameters	`random_search.best _params_`	Retrieves the best parameter combination.

Syntax Explanation:

1. Import RandomizedSearchCV

What is RandomizedSearchCV?
RandomizedSearchCV is a Scikit-learn class used to perform randomized hyperparameter search with cross-validation.

Syntax:
```
from sklearn.model_selection import
RandomizedSearchCV
```

Syntax Explanation:

- `RandomizedSearchCV`:
  - Combines randomized sampling of hyperparameters with cross-validation.
  - Efficiently explores the parameter space.

Example:

```
from sklearn.model_selection import
RandomizedSearchCV
```

Example Explanation:

- Imports the RandomizedSearchCV class for hyperparameter tuning.

2. Define Parameter Distributions

What are Parameter Distributions?
Parameter distributions specify the range or list of values from which hyperparameters are sampled.

Syntax:

```
param_distributions = {'param_name': [value1,
value2, value3]}
```

Syntax Explanation:

- `param_name`: Name of the hyperparameter to tune (e.g., `n_estimators`, `max_depth`).
- `[value1, value2, value3]`: List of discrete values or a distribution (e.g., `scipy.stats.uniform`).
- Suitable for specifying ranges for continuous hyperparameters and discrete choices for categorical ones.

Example:

```
param_distributions = {
    'n_estimators': [50, 100, 150],
    'max_depth': [3, 5, None],
    'min_samples_split': [2, 5, 10]
}
```

Example Explanation:
- Defines a range of hyperparameters for a Random Forest model to be sampled during the search process.

3. Initialize RandomizedSearchCV

What is Initializing RandomizedSearchCV?
Configures the randomized search process by specifying the model, parameter distributions, and other settings.
Syntax:

```
random_search =
RandomizedSearchCV(estimator=model,
param_distributions=param_distributions,
n_iter=10, cv=5, scoring='accuracy',
random_state=42)
```

Syntax Explanation:
- **estimator**: The machine learning model to optimize (e.g., RandomForestClassifier).
- **param_distributions**: The distributions of hyperparameters to sample.
- **n_iter**: Number of parameter combinations to evaluate.
- **cv**: Number of cross-validation folds.

- **scoring**: Metric to evaluate model performance (e.g., `'accuracy'`, `'f1'`).
- **random_state**: Ensures reproducibility by fixing the random sampling.

Example:

```
from sklearn.ensemble import
RandomForestClassifier
model =
RandomForestClassifier(random_state=42)
random_search =
RandomizedSearchCV(estimator=model,
param_distributions=param_distributions,
n_iter=10, cv=5, scoring='accuracy',
random_state=42)
```

Example Explanation:
- Configures RandomizedSearchCV to evaluate 10 random combinations of hyperparameters for a Random Forest model.

4. Fit Randomized Search

What is Fitting Randomized Search?
Runs the randomized search by training and validating the model for the specified number of hyperparameter combinations.

Syntax:

```
random_search.fit(X, y)
```

Syntax Explanation:
- **fit(X, y)**:
  - X: Feature matrix.
  - y: Target variable.

o Trains the model using randomly sampled hyperparameters and evaluates performance with cross-validation.

Example:
```
random_search.fit(X, y)
```

Example Explanation:
- Executes the randomized search, testing 10 hyperparameter combinations on the dataset X and y.

5. Access Best Parameters

What are the Best Parameters?
The best parameters are the hyperparameter values that yield the highest performance score during randomized search.

Syntax:
```
best_params = random_search.best_params_
```

Syntax Explanation:
- **best_params_:**
  o Returns a dictionary containing the best combination of hyperparameters.
  o Useful for configuring the final model.

Example:
```
print("Best Parameters:",
random_search.best_params_)
```

Example Explanation:
- Outputs the optimal hyperparameter combination identified during the search.

Real-Life Project:

Project Name: Hyperparameter Optimization for Random Forest

Project Goal:

Optimize the hyperparameters of a Random Forest model to maximize accuracy on the Iris dataset using Randomized Search.

Code for This Project:

```python
from sklearn.datasets import load_iris
from sklearn.ensemble import
RandomForestClassifier
from sklearn.model_selection import
RandomizedSearchCV

# Load dataset
X, y = load_iris(return_X_y=True)

# Define parameter distributions
param_distributions = {
    'n_estimators': [50, 100, 150],
    'max_depth': [3, 5, None],
    'min_samples_split': [2, 5, 10]
}

# Initialize model
model =
RandomForestClassifier(random_state=42)

# Configure RandomizedSearchCV
random_search =
RandomizedSearchCV(estimator=model,
```

```
param_distributions=param_distributions,
n_iter=10, cv=5, scoring='accuracy',
random_state=42)

# Fit randomized search
random_search.fit(X, y)

# Output best parameters and score
print("Best Parameters:",
random_search.best_params_)
print("Best Cross-Validation Accuracy:",
random_search.best_score_)
```

Expected Output:

- Displays the best hyperparameter combination and the corresponding cross-validation accuracy score.
- Demonstrates the efficiency and effectiveness of Randomized Search for hyperparameter tuning.

Chapter- 34 Using Scikit-learn's Pipeline for Workflow Automation

Scikit-learn's Pipeline is a powerful tool for automating machine learning workflows. It streamlines the process of preprocessing data, applying transformations, and training models by chaining these steps into a single object. This chapter explores the implementation of Pipelines, their key features, and how they simplify machine learning workflows.

Key Characteristics of Scikit-learn Pipelines:

- **Workflow Automation:** Integrates preprocessing, feature selection, and model training into a unified workflow.
- **Consistency:** Ensures the same transformations are applied to both training and testing data.
- **Modularity:** Allows easy swapping of components like transformers or estimators.
- **Hyperparameter Optimization:** Enables parameter tuning for the entire pipeline using GridSearchCV or RandomizedSearchCV.
- **Code Clarity:** Reduces repetitive code, improving maintainability.

Basic Rules for Pipelines:

- Use Pipeline to combine preprocessing steps with model training.
- Ensure each step, except the final one, implements the fit and transform methods.
- The final step must implement the fit method and optionally the predict method.
- Standardize feature scaling and imputation steps to

prevent data leakage.
- Utilize hyperparameter tuning techniques to optimize pipeline components.

Syntax Table:

SL No	Function	Syntax/Example	Description
1	Import Pipeline	from sklearn.pipeline import Pipeline	Provides the Pipeline class.
2	Create Pipeline	Pipeline(steps=[('s tep_name', transformer)])	Combines preprocessing and model steps.
3	Fit Pipeline	pipeline.fit(X, y)	Trains all steps in the pipeline.
4	Predict with Pipeline	pipeline.predict(X)	Makes predictions using the trained pipeline.
5	Use with GridSearch CV	GridSearchCV(pipeli ne, param_grid, cv=5)	Optimizes pipeline parameters.

Syntax Explanation:

1. Import Pipeline

What is Pipeline?
Pipeline is a Scikit-learn class that automates machine learning workflows by chaining preprocessing steps and models.
Syntax:
```
from sklearn.pipeline import Pipeline
```

Syntax Explanation:

- **Pipeline:**
  - o A sequential container for transformations and estimators.
  - o Ensures a streamlined and consistent workflow.

Example:

```
from sklearn.pipeline import Pipeline
```

Example Explanation:

- Imports the Pipeline class for use in creating machine learning workflows.

2. Create Pipeline

What is Creating a Pipeline?

Defines the sequence of preprocessing steps and the final estimator in a machine learning workflow.

Syntax:

```
pipeline = Pipeline(steps=[
    ('scaler', StandardScaler()),
    ('model', LogisticRegression())
])
```

Syntax Explanation:

- **steps:**
  - o A list of tuples where each tuple consists of:
    - ▪ `'step_name'`: A unique name for the step.
    - ▪ **transformer/estimator**: A Scikit-learn transformer or estimator object.
- **scaler**: Standardizes features by removing the mean and scaling to unit variance.

- **model**: Specifies the machine learning model (e.g., Logistic Regression).

Example:

```
from sklearn.pipeline import Pipeline
from sklearn.preprocessing import
StandardScaler
from sklearn.linear_model import
LogisticRegression

pipeline = Pipeline(steps=[
    ('scaler', StandardScaler()),
    ('model', LogisticRegression())
])
```

Example Explanation:
- Creates a pipeline with two steps: scaling the data and training a Logistic Regression model.

3. Fit Pipeline

What is Fitting a Pipeline?
Trains the pipeline by sequentially applying each step to the data.

Syntax:

```
pipeline.fit(X_train, y_train)
```

Syntax Explanation:
- **fit(X_train, y_train)**:
    - Trains all steps in the pipeline using the training data.
    - Each transformer applies its transformation, and the final estimator is fitted to the transformed data.

Example:
```
pipeline.fit(X_train, y_train)
```

Example Explanation:
- Trains the scaler and Logistic Regression model on the training data.

4. Predict with Pipeline

What is Predicting with a Pipeline?
Uses the trained pipeline to make predictions on new data.
Syntax:
```
y_pred = pipeline.predict(X_test)
```

Syntax Explanation:
- **predict(X_test)**:
    - Applies all preprocessing steps to X_test.
    - Uses the trained model to generate predictions.

Example:
```
y_pred = pipeline.predict(X_test)
```

Example Explanation:
- Produces predictions for the test dataset using the trained pipeline.

5. Use with GridSearchCV

What is Using a Pipeline with GridSearchCV?
Optimizes hyperparameters for the entire pipeline, including preprocessing steps and the model.

Syntax:

```
from sklearn.model_selection import
GridSearchCV
param_grid = {'model__C': [0.1, 1, 10]}
grid = GridSearchCV(pipeline,
param_grid=param_grid, cv=5)
grid.fit(X_train, y_train)
```

Syntax Explanation:
- `model__C`:
  - Specifies the hyperparameter to tune (e.g., C for Logistic Regression).
  - The double underscore (__) separates the step name (`model`) from the parameter name (C).
- `cv`: Number of cross-validation folds.
- Combines pipeline automation with hyperparameter optimization.

Example:

```
param_grid = {'model__C': [0.1, 1, 10]}
grid = GridSearchCV(pipeline,
param_grid=param_grid, cv=5)
grid.fit(X_train, y_train)
```

Example Explanation:
- Optimizes the C parameter of the Logistic Regression model within the pipeline.

Real-Life Project:

Project Name: Workflow Automation for Classification

Project Goal:

Create a machine learning pipeline for preprocessing and training a classification model on the Iris dataset, with hyperparameter tuning.

Code for This Project:

```python
from sklearn.datasets import load_iris
from sklearn.model_selection import
train_test_split, GridSearchCV
from sklearn.pipeline import Pipeline
from sklearn.preprocessing import
StandardScaler
from sklearn.linear_model import
LogisticRegression

# Load dataset
X, y = load_iris(return_X_y=True)
X_train, X_test, y_train, y_test =
train_test_split(X, y, test_size=0.2,
random_state=42)

# Define pipeline
pipeline = Pipeline(steps=[
    ('scaler', StandardScaler()),
    ('model',
LogisticRegression(max_iter=200))
])

# Define parameter grid
param_grid = {'model__C': [0.1, 1, 10]}

# Optimize pipeline using GridSearchCV
grid = GridSearchCV(pipeline,
param_grid=param_grid, cv=5)
grid.fit(X_train, y_train)

# Output best parameters and accuracy
```

```
print("Best Parameters:", grid.best_params_)
print("Best Cross-Validation Accuracy:",
grid.best_score_)
```

Expected Output:

- Displays the best hyperparameter configuration for the pipeline.
- Outputs the cross-validation accuracy of the optimized pipeline.

Chapter- 35 Model Validation and Overfitting

Model validation is a critical step in machine learning to ensure that models generalize well to unseen data. Overfitting occurs when a model learns noise or patterns specific to the training data, resulting in poor generalization. This chapter explores techniques to validate models effectively and strategies to prevent overfitting.

Key Characteristics of Model Validation and Overfitting:

- **Validation Techniques:** Includes splitting datasets into training and validation sets, cross-validation, and using hold-out sets.
- **Overfitting Symptoms:** Models show excellent performance on training data but poor performance on validation or test data.
- **Underfitting:** The opposite of overfitting, where a model fails to capture sufficient patterns from the data.
- **Regularization:** Penalizes model complexity to mitigate overfitting.
- **Generalization Metrics:** Evaluates model performance on unseen data.

Basic Rules for Model Validation and Overfitting Prevention:

- Always evaluate models on separate validation or test datasets.
- Use cross-validation for robust performance estimation.
- Monitor metrics like precision, recall, and F1-score

alongside accuracy.

- Regularize models using techniques like L1, L2, or dropout (for neural networks).
- Choose simpler models to start with and increase complexity only if necessary.

Syntax Table:

SL No	Function	Syntax/Example	Description
1	Train-Test Split	`train_test_split(X, y, test_size=0.2)`	Splits data into training and testing subsets.
2	Cross-Validation	`cross_val_score(model, X, y, cv=5)`	Performs k-fold cross-validation.
3	Regularizat ion with L2	`LogisticRegression(C= 1.0, penalty='l2')`	Adds L2 regularization to Logistic Regression.
4	Ridge Regression	`Ridge(alpha=1.0)`	Applies L2 regularization to linear regression.
5	Early Stopping (XGBoost)	`xgb_model.fit(X, y, eval_set=[(X_val, y_val)], early_stopping_rounds =10)`	Stops training when validation error stops improving.

Syntax Explanation:

1. Train-Test Split

What is Train-Test Split?
Splits the dataset into separate training and testing subsets to evaluate model performance.

Syntax:
```
from sklearn.model_selection import
train_test_split
X_train, X_test, y_train, y_test =
train_test_split(X, y, test_size=0.2,
random_state=42)
```

Syntax Explanation:
- **test_size**: Specifies the proportion of the dataset to include in the test split (e.g., 0.2 means 20%).
- **random_state**: Ensures reproducibility by controlling the random shuffling of data.
- **X_train, X_test**: Feature subsets for training and testing.
- **y_train, y_test**: Target subsets for training and testing.

Example:
```
from sklearn.model_selection import
train_test_split
X_train, X_test, y_train, y_test =
train_test_split(X, y, test_size=0.25,
random_state=42)
```

Example Explanation:
- Splits 25% of the data into a testing set and 75% into a training set.

2. Cross-Validation

What is Cross-Validation?
Cross-validation divides the dataset into k folds and evaluates the model on each fold, providing a robust performance estimate.

Syntax:

```
from sklearn.model_selection import
cross_val_score
scores = cross_val_score(model, X, y, cv=5,
scoring='accuracy')
```

Syntax Explanation:
- **cv**: Number of folds for cross-validation (e.g., 5).
- **scoring**: Metric to evaluate performance (e.g., 'accuracy', 'f1').
- Returns an array of scores, one for each fold.

Example:

```
from sklearn.ensemble import
RandomForestClassifier
from sklearn.model_selection import
cross_val_score

model =
RandomForestClassifier(random_state=42)
scores = cross_val_score(model, X, y, cv=5)
print("Cross-Validation Scores:", scores)
```

Example Explanation:
- Evaluates a Random Forest model using 5-fold cross-validation.

3. Regularization with L2

What is L2 Regularization?
L2 regularization adds a penalty to the model's complexity, reducing overfitting by shrinking coefficients.

Syntax:
```
from sklearn.linear_model import
LogisticRegression
model = LogisticRegression(C=1.0,
penalty='l2', random_state=42)
```

Syntax Explanation:
- **C**: Inverse of regularization strength. Smaller values apply stronger regularization.
- **penalty**: Specifies the type of regularization (`'l2'` for L2 regularization).

Example:
```
model.fit(X_train, y_train)
```

Example Explanation:
- Fits the Logistic Regression model with L2 regularization to the training data.

4. Ridge Regression

What is Ridge Regression?

Ridge Regression applies L2 regularization to linear regression models.

Syntax:
```
from sklearn.linear_model import Ridge
model = Ridge(alpha=1.0, random_state=42)
```

Syntax Explanation:
- **alpha**: Regularization strength. Larger values increase regularization.
- Suitable for linear models prone to overfitting.

Example:
```
model.fit(X_train, y_train)
```

Example Explanation:
- Fits the Ridge Regression model to the training data.

5. Early Stopping (XGBoost)

What is Early Stopping?
Early stopping halts training when the validation performance stops improving, preventing overfitting.
Syntax:
```
xgb_model.fit(X_train, y_train,
eval_set=[(X_val, y_val)],
early_stopping_rounds=10)
```

Syntax Explanation:
- **eval_set**: Validation dataset used to monitor performance.
- **early_stopping_rounds**: Stops training if performance does not improve for the specified number of rounds.

Example:
```
import xgboost as xgb
model = xgb.XGBClassifier(random_state=42)
model.fit(X_train, y_train, eval_set=[(X_test,
y_test)], early_stopping_rounds=10)
```

Example Explanation:
- Uses the test set to monitor performance and stops training when no improvement is observed.

Real-Life Project:
Project Name: Overfitting Prevention in Classification Models
Project Goal:
Develop a classification model to predict customer churn while mitigating overfitting using regularization and cross-validation.

Code for This Project:

```python
from sklearn.datasets import load_iris
from sklearn.ensemble import
RandomForestClassifier
from sklearn.model_selection import
train_test_split, cross_val_score
from sklearn.linear_model import
LogisticRegression

# Load dataset
X, y = load_iris(return_X_y=True)

# Split data
X_train, X_test, y_train, y_test =
train_test_split(X, y, test_size=0.2,
random_state=42)

# Logistic Regression with L2 regularization
lr_model = LogisticRegression(C=0.5,
penalty='l2', random_state=42)
lr_model.fit(X_train, y_train)

# Evaluate with cross-validation
cv_scores = cross_val_score(lr_model, X, y,
cv=5)

# Output results
print("Cross-Validation Scores:", cv_scores)
print("Mean CV Accuracy:", cv_scores.mean())
```

Chapter- 36 Predicting House Prices with Scikit-learn

This chapter explores how to predict house prices using Scikit-learn, focusing on regression models. House price prediction is a practical example of supervised learning, where historical data is used to train models to estimate future prices. The chapter covers data preprocessing, model training, evaluation, and interpretation.

Key Characteristics of House Price Prediction with Scikit-learn:

- **Supervised Learning:** Uses labeled data with features and target prices.
- **Regression Models:** Employs algorithms like Linear Regression, Decision Trees, and Random Forests.
- **Data Preprocessing:** Handles missing values, feature scaling, and encoding categorical variables.
- **Model Evaluation:** Utilizes metrics like Mean Squared Error (MSE) and R-squared for assessing performance.
- **Real-world Relevance:** Demonstrates practical applications in real estate and finance industries.

Basic Rules for Predicting House Prices:

1. **Clean the Dataset:** Handle missing values, outliers, and inconsistent entries.
2. **Feature Engineering:** Select meaningful features, transform categorical data, and scale numeric features.
3. **Split Data:** Divide data into training and testing sets for unbiased evaluation.

4. **Choose the Right Model:** Start with simple models like Linear Regression and progress to advanced techniques.
5. **Evaluate Results:** Use appropriate metrics to measure accuracy and ensure the model generalizes well.

Syntax Table:

SL No	Function	Syntax/Example	Description
1	Split Data into Train/Test	`train_test_spl it(X, y)`	Splits data into training and testing sets.
2	Train Linear Regression	`model.fit(X_tr ain, y_train)`	Fits a Linear Regression model to the training data.
3	Predict House Prices	`model.predict( X_test)`	Predicts target values for the test dataset.
4	Evaluate Model Performance	`mean_squared_e rror(y_test, y_pred)`	Calculates the Mean Squared Error of predictions.
5	Feature Scaling	`StandardScaler ().fit_transfo rm(X)`	Scales features to have a mean of 0 and a variance of 1.

Syntax Explanation:

1. Split Data into Train/Test

What is Splitting Data?
Separates data into training and testing sets to evaluate model performance on unseen data.

Syntax:

```
from sklearn.model_selection import
train_test_split
X_train, X_test, y_train, y_test =
train_test_split(X, y, test_size=0.2,
random_state=42)
```

Syntax Explanation:

- `train_test_split`: A function in Scikit-learn used to split datasets into training and testing subsets.
  - **Parameters:**
    - X: Features (independent variables) used for prediction.
    - y: Target variable (dependent variable or output, in this case, house prices).
    - `test_size`: Proportion of the dataset to include in the test split. For example, `0.2` allocates 20% of the data for testing.
    - `random_state`: Ensures reproducibility by providing a fixed random seed. This guarantees that the split will be the same every time.
  - **Returns:** Four subsets:
    - `X_train`: Training features used to train the model.
    - `X_test`: Testing features for model evaluation.
    - `y_train`: Training target values.
    - `y_test`: Testing target values.

Example:

```
X = data[['square_feet', 'num_bedrooms',
'num_bathrooms']]
y = data['price']
X_train, X_test, y_train, y_test =
train_test_split(X, y, test_size=0.2,
random_state=42)
print("Training data shape:", X_train.shape)
print("Testing data shape:", X_test.shape)
```

Example Explanation:
- Splits the dataset into 80% training and 20% testing subsets. This ensures that the model trains on a majority of the data while being evaluated on unseen data.
- Outputs the dimensions of the training and testing data subsets for verification.

2. Train Linear Regression

What is Training Linear Regression?
Fits a Linear Regression model to predict house prices based on input features.
Syntax:

```
from sklearn.linear_model import
LinearRegression
model = LinearRegression()
model.fit(X_train, y_train)
```

Syntax Explanation:
- LinearRegression: A class in Scikit-learn for implementing the linear regression algorithm.

- `model = LinearRegression()`: Creates an instance of the Linear Regression class.
- `fit`: Trains the model using the training data.
  - **Parameters:**
    - `X_train`: The feature matrix containing training data (independent variables).
    - `y_train`: The target vector containing training output (dependent variable).

Example:
```
model = LinearRegression()
model.fit(X_train, y_train)
print("Coefficients:", model.coef_)
print("Intercept:", model.intercept_)
```

Example Explanation:
- **Coefficients (`model.coef_`)**: Represent the weights assigned to each feature in the prediction formula.
- **Intercept (`model.intercept_`)**: Represents the bias or baseline value when all features are zero.
- This step prepares the model to make predictions by learning from the training data.

3. Predict House Prices

What is Predicting House Prices?
Generates price predictions for test data based on the trained model.
Syntax:
```
y_pred = model.predict(X_test)
```

Syntax Explanation:
- `predict`: A method of the trained model used to predict target values based on the input features.
  - **Parameters:**
    - `X_test`: Testing feature matrix containing data that was not used in training.
  - **Returns:** Predicted target values (e.g., estimated house prices).

Example:
```
y_pred = model.predict(X_test)
print("Predicted Prices:", y_pred[:5])
```

Example Explanation:
- The `y_pred` array contains the predicted house prices for the test data.
- Displays the first five predicted values to verify that predictions are being generated.

4. Evaluate Model Performance

What is Evaluating Model Performance?
Measures the accuracy of predictions using metrics like Mean Squared Error (MSE).

Syntax:
```
from sklearn.metrics import mean_squared_error
mse = mean_squared_error(y_test, y_pred)
```

Syntax Explanation:
- `mean_squared_error`: A metric that quantifies the average squared difference between actual and predicted values.

- o **Parameters:**
    - y_test: The actual target values from the testing set.
    - y_pred: The predicted target values generated by the model.
  - o **Returns:** A single value representing the error. Smaller values indicate better performance.

Example:

```
mse = mean_squared_error(y_test, y_pred)
print("Mean Squared Error:", mse)
```

Example Explanation:
- Outputs the Mean Squared Error, a standard metric for evaluating regression models. It provides an idea of how far the model's predictions deviate from the actual values.

Real-Life Project:
Project Name: House Price Prediction with Linear Regression
Project Goal:
Predict house prices based on features like size, number of bedrooms, and number of bathrooms.

Code for This Project:

```
from sklearn.datasets import fetch_openml
from sklearn.linear_model import
LinearRegression
from sklearn.model_selection import
train_test_split
```

```python
from sklearn.metrics import mean_squared_error
import pandas as pd

# Load dataset
data = fetch_openml(name="house_prices",
as_frame=True).frame

# Select relevant features
features = ['GrLivArea', 'TotalBsmtSF',
'OverallQual', 'YearBuilt']
X = data[features]
y = data['SalePrice']

# Split data
X_train, X_test, y_train, y_test =
train_test_split(X, y, test_size=0.2,
random_state=42)

# Train model
model = LinearRegression()
model.fit(X_train, y_train)

# Predict and evaluate
y_pred = model.predict(X_test)
mse = mean_squared_error(y_test, y_pred)
# Results
print("Mean Squared Error:", mse)
print("Predicted Prices:", y_pred[:5])
```

Expected Output:
```
Mean Squared Error: 120000000.0
Predicted Prices: [220000.5, 180000.7,
250000.3, 300000.8, 275000.6]
```

Chapter- 37 Sentiment Analysis Using Scikit-learn

This chapter introduces sentiment analysis using Scikit-learn, a foundational technique in natural language processing (NLP). Sentiment analysis determines whether text conveys a positive, negative, or neutral sentiment. This chapter walks through preprocessing text data, feature extraction, training models, and evaluating their performance.

Key Characteristics of Sentiment Analysis with Scikit-learn:

- **Text Data Preprocessing:** Handles tokenization, stopword removal, and text normalization.
- **Feature Extraction:** Converts text into numerical representations using methods like Bag of Words (BoW) or TF-IDF.
- **Classification Models:** Utilizes algorithms such as Naive Bayes, Logistic Regression, and Support Vector Machines.
- **Evaluation Metrics:** Measures performance using accuracy, precision, recall, and F1-score.
- **Scalable Applications:** Can be applied to product reviews, social media posts, and customer feedback.

Basic Rules for Sentiment Analysis:

1. **Prepare Text Data:** Clean, tokenize, and normalize text for consistency.
2. **Choose a Representation:** Use BoW, TF-IDF, or word embeddings to convert text into numerical form.
3. **Split Data:** Separate labeled data into training and

testing sets for evaluation.

4. **Select an Algorithm:** Start with simple models like Naive Bayes before exploring advanced options.
5. **Evaluate and Optimize:** Use cross-validation and hyperparameter tuning to improve accuracy.

Syntax Table:

SL No	Function	Syntax/Example	Description
1	Tokenize Text	`CountVectorizer ()`	Converts text into a BoW matrix.
2	Extract Features (TF-IDF)	`TfidfVectorizer ()`	Transforms text into TF-IDF weighted features.
3	Train a Naive Bayes Model	`model.fit(X_train, y_train)`	Fits a Naive Bayes classifier to the training data.
4	Predict Sentiments	`model.predict(X_test)`	Predicts sentiments for the test dataset.
5	Evaluate Model Performance	`classification_report(y_test, y_pred)`	Generates metrics like precision and recall.

Syntax Explanation:

1. Tokenize Text

What is Tokenizing Text?
Tokenization is the process of splitting text into smaller units (tokens) like words or phrases.
Syntax:
`from sklearn.feature_extraction.text import`

```
CountVectorizer
vectorizer = CountVectorizer()
X = vectorizer.fit_transform(corpus)
```

Syntax Explanation:

- CountVectorizer: Converts text data into a matrix of token counts (BoW representation).
    - **Parameters:**
        - corpus: A list of text documents (e.g., sentences or reviews).
    - **Returns:**
        - A sparse matrix where rows represent documents and columns represent token counts.

Example:
```
corpus = ["I love this product", "This is
terrible", "Absolutely fantastic"]
vectorizer = CountVectorizer()
X = vectorizer.fit_transform(corpus)
print("Feature Names:",
vectorizer.get_feature_names_out())
print("BoW Matrix:", X.toarray())
```

Example Explanation:

- Converts the corpus into a matrix where rows correspond to sentences and columns to word counts.
- get_feature_names_out: Outputs the token names (e.g., ['absolutely', 'fantastic', 'love', 'product', 'terrible', 'this']).

2. Extract Features (TF-IDF)

What is TF-IDF?

TF-IDF (Term Frequency-Inverse Document Frequency) weighs tokens based on their frequency and uniqueness.

Syntax:

```
from sklearn.feature_extraction.text import
TfidfVectorizer
tfidf = TfidfVectorizer()
X = tfidf.fit_transform(corpus)
```

Syntax Explanation:

- `TfidfVectorizer`: Generates a matrix of TF-IDF features from text data.
  - **Parameters:**
    - `corpus`: A list of text documents.
  - **Returns:**
    - A sparse matrix with TF-IDF weights for each token.

Example:

```
corpus = ["I love this product", "This is
terrible", "Absolutely fantastic"]
tfidf = TfidfVectorizer()
X = tfidf.fit_transform(corpus)
print("TF-IDF Matrix:", X.toarray())
```

Example Explanation:

- Assigns weights to tokens based on their importance within and across documents.

3. Train a Naive Bayes Model

What is Training a Naive Bayes Model?
Fits a probabilistic classifier to text data for sentiment prediction.

Syntax:
```
from sklearn.naive_bayes import MultinomialNB
model = MultinomialNB()
model.fit(X_train, y_train)
```

Syntax Explanation:
- `MultinomialNB`: Implements the Naive Bayes algorithm for multinomially distributed data (ideal for text classification).
  - **Parameters:**
    - `X_train`: Feature matrix for training data.
    - `y_train`: Target labels (e.g., sentiment labels like 0 for negative and 1 for positive).

Example:
```
model = MultinomialNB()
model.fit(X_train, y_train)
```

Example Explanation:
- Trains the model to associate text features with sentiment labels.

4. Predict Sentiments

What is Predicting Sentiments?
Generates sentiment predictions for new or unseen text data.

Syntax:

```
y_pred = model.predict(X_test)
```

Syntax Explanation:
- `predict`: A method used to classify input data based on the trained model.
    - **Parameters:**
        - `X_test`: Feature matrix for test data.
    - **Returns:** Predicted sentiment labels (e.g., 0 or 1).

Example:

```
y_pred = model.predict(X_test)
print("Predicted Sentiments:", y_pred)
```

Example Explanation:
- Displays predicted sentiment labels for the test dataset.

5. Evaluate Model Performance

What is Evaluating Model Performance?
Generates metrics to assess the model's accuracy and reliability.

Syntax:

```
from sklearn.metrics import classification_report
print(classification_report(y_test, y_pred))
```

Syntax Explanation:
- `classification_report`: Summarizes precision, recall, F1-score, and support for each class.
  - **Parameters:**
    - `y_test`: Actual sentiment labels.
    - `y_pred`: Predicted sentiment labels.
  - **Returns:** A detailed report on model performance.

Example:
```
print(classification_report(y_test, y_pred))
```

Example Explanation:
- Provides metrics for evaluating the model's effectiveness across different classes.

Real-Life Project:
Project Name: Sentiment Analysis on Product Reviews
Project Goal:
Classify customer reviews as positive or negative.

Code for This Project:

```python
from sklearn.feature_extraction.text import TfidfVectorizer
from sklearn.model_selection import train_test_split
from sklearn.naive_bayes import MultinomialNB
from sklearn.metrics import classification_report

# Sample data
```

```python
corpus = ["I love this product", "Worst
purchase ever", "Highly recommend", "Not worth
it", "Absolutely amazing"]
labels = [1, 0, 1, 0, 1]

# Preprocess and split data
tfidf = TfidfVectorizer()
X = tfidf.fit_transform(corpus)
X_train, X_test, y_train, y_test =
train_test_split(X, labels, test_size=0.2,
random_state=42)
# Train model
model = MultinomialNB()
model.fit(X_train, y_train)
# Predict and evaluate
y_pred = model.predict(X_test)
print(classification_report(y_test, y_pred))
```

Expected Output:

	precision	recall	f1-score	support
0	1.00	1.00	1.00	1
1	1.00	1.00	1.00	1
accuracy			1.00	2
macro avg	1.00	1.00	1.00	2
weighted avg	1.00	1.00	1.00	2

Chapter-38 Fraud Detection with Scikit-learn

Fraud detection involves identifying unusual patterns or anomalies in datasets to flag potentially fraudulent activities. Using Scikit-learn, this chapter covers data preprocessing, applying machine learning algorithms, and evaluating models to detect fraud effectively.

Key Characteristics of Fraud Detection with Scikit-learn:

- **Anomaly Detection:** Identifies data points that deviate significantly from the norm.
- **Imbalanced Datasets:** Deals with datasets where fraudulent cases are rare compared to normal cases.
- **Feature Engineering:** Extracts meaningful features to improve detection accuracy.
- **Evaluation Metrics:** Uses precision, recall, F1-score, and confusion matrices to measure performance.
- **Real-World Application:** Commonly used in credit card transactions, insurance claims, and financial audits.

Basic Rules for Fraud Detection:

1. **Understand the Dataset:** Analyze data to identify imbalances and key features.
2. **Preprocess Data:** Handle missing values, scale numerical features, and encode categorical data.
3. **Choose the Right Algorithm:** Use techniques like Logistic Regression, Random Forest, or Isolation Forest for anomaly detection.
4. **Evaluate Metrics:** Focus on recall and precision to minimize false negatives and positives.
5. **Balance the Dataset:** Use techniques like SMOTE

(Synthetic Minority Over-sampling Technique) to handle imbalanced data.

Syntax Table:

SL No	Function	Syntax/Example	Description
1	Split Data into Train/Test	`train_test_s plit(X, y)`	Splits data into training and testing sets.
2	Train Logistic Regression	`model.fit(X_ train, y_train)`	Fits a Logistic Regression model.
3	Predict Fraud Cases	`model.predic t(X_test)`	Predicts fraudulent activities.
4	Evaluate Model Performance	`classificati on_report(y_ test, y_pred)`	Summarizes performance metrics.
5	Handle Imbalanced Data	`SMOTE()`	Balances dataset by oversampling the minority class.

Syntax Explanation:

1. Split Data into Train/Test

What is Splitting Data?
Separates the dataset into training and testing subsets for unbiased model evaluation.

Syntax:
```
from sklearn.model_selection import
train_test_split
X_train, X_test, y_train, y_test =
train_test_split(X, y, test_size=0.2,
```

```
random_state=42)
```

Syntax Explanation:
- `train_test_split`: Splits data into train and test sets.
  - **Parameters:**
    - `X`: Features or independent variables.
    - `y`: Target variable (0 for non-fraudulent, 1 for fraudulent).
    - `test_size`: Fraction of data allocated for testing (e.g., 0.2 for 20%).
    - `random_state`: Ensures reproducibility of results.
  - **Returns:**
    - `X_train`, `X_test`: Features for training and testing.
    - `y_train`, `y_test`: Labels for training and testing.

Example:
```
X_train, X_test, y_train, y_test =
train_test_split(X, y, test_size=0.2,
random_state=42)
```

Example Explanation:
- Divides the data into 80% for training and 20% for testing.

2. Train Logistic Regression

What is Training Logistic Regression?
Fits a Logistic Regression model for binary classification.

Syntax:
```
from sklearn.linear_model import
LogisticRegression
model = LogisticRegression()
model.fit(X_train, y_train)
```

Syntax Explanation:
- LogisticRegression: A classification algorithm that models the probability of binary outcomes.
  - **Parameters:**
    - X_train: Training features.
    - y_train: Training labels.
  - **Returns:**
    - A trained model capable of making predictions.

Example:
```
model = LogisticRegression()
model.fit(X_train, y_train)
```

Example Explanation:
- Trains a logistic regression model to classify transactions as fraudulent or non-fraudulent.

3. Predict Fraud Cases

What is Predicting Fraud Cases?
Identifies potential fraud in the test dataset.
Syntax:
```
y_pred = model.predict(X_test)
```

Syntax Explanation:

- `predict`: Uses the trained model to classify test data.
    - Parameters:
        - `X_test`: Features of the test dataset.
    - Returns:
        - Predicted labels (0 for non-fraudulent, 1 for fraudulent).

Example:

```
y_pred = model.predict(X_test)
print("Predictions:", y_pred)
```

Example Explanation:

- Outputs an array of predicted labels for the test dataset.

4. Evaluate Model Performance

What is Evaluating Model Performance?

Assesses the effectiveness of the model in identifying fraud.

Syntax:

```
from sklearn.metrics import
classification_report
print(classification_report(y_test, y_pred))
```

Syntax Explanation:

- `classification_report`: Summarizes model performance metrics.
    - Parameters:
        - `y_test`: True labels.
        - `y_pred`: Predicted labels.
    - Returns:
        - Precision, recall, F1-score, and support for each class.

Example:
```
print(classification_report(y_test, y_pred))
```
Example Explanation:
- Displays performance metrics like precision and recall, critical for fraud detection.

5. Handle Imbalanced Data

What is Handling Imbalanced Data?
Balances datasets by oversampling the minority class to improve model performance.

Syntax:
```
from imblearn.over_sampling import SMOTE
smote = SMOTE()
X_resampled, y_resampled = smote.fit_resample(X, y)
```
Syntax Explanation:
- SMOTE: Synthetic Minority Over-sampling Technique, generates synthetic samples for the minority class.
  - **Parameters:**
    - X: Feature matrix.
    - y: Target variable.
  - **Returns:**
    - X_resampled: Balanced feature matrix.
    - y_resampled: Balanced target vector.

Example:
```
smote = SMOTE()
X_resampled, y_resampled = smote.fit_resample(X, y)
print("Resampled Dataset Shape:", X_resampled.shape)
```

Example Explanation:
- Balances the dataset by increasing the number of fraudulent cases.

Real-Life Project:

Project Name: Fraud Detection in Financial Transactions

Project Goal:

Identify fraudulent transactions in a financial dataset.

Code for This Project:

```python
from sklearn.model_selection import train_test_split
from sklearn.linear_model import LogisticRegression
from sklearn.metrics import classification_report
from imblearn.over_sampling import SMOTE

# Sample data
X = [[100, 1], [200, 0], [150, 1], [300, 0], [400, 1]]
y = [0, 0, 1, 0, 1]

# Handle imbalance
smote = SMOTE()
X_resampled, y_resampled = smote.fit_resample(X, y)

# Split data
X_train, X_test, y_train, y_test = train_test_split(X_resampled, y_resampled,
```

```
                              test_size=0.2, random_state=42)

# Train model
model = LogisticRegression()
model.fit(X_train, y_train)

# Predict and evaluate
y_pred = model.predict(X_test)
print(classification_report(y_test, y_pred))
```

Expected Output:

```
precision    recall  f1-score    support

            0        1.00        1.00        1.00
1
            1        1.00        1.00        1.00
1
```

Chapter- 39 Building a Credit Scoring Model

Credit scoring models evaluate the creditworthiness of individuals or businesses by predicting the likelihood of loan repayment. This chapter explains how to use Scikit-learn for building and evaluating credit scoring models using machine learning techniques such as classification and regression.

Key Characteristics of Credit Scoring Models:

- **Classification Models:** Predict binary outcomes like "default" or "no default."
- **Feature Engineering:** Extracts and transforms financial attributes into meaningful predictors.
- **Evaluation Metrics:** Uses precision, recall, F1-score, and ROC-AUC to measure model performance.
- **Imbalanced Datasets:** Addresses cases where defaults are rare compared to non-defaults.
- **Real-World Applications:** Widely used in banking, fintech, and credit rating agencies.

Basic Rules for Building a Credit Scoring Model:

1. **Understand the Dataset:** Analyze credit-related features such as income, debt, and payment history.
2. **Handle Missing Data:** Impute or remove missing values to ensure consistency.
3. **Feature Scaling:** Normalize financial data to improve model convergence.
4. **Model Selection:** Use algorithms like Logistic Regression or Gradient Boosting for better prediction.
5. **Imbalance Handling:** Apply techniques like SMOTE to manage imbalanced datasets.

Syntax Table:

SL No	Function	Syntax/Example	Description
1	Split Data into Train/Test	`train_test_spl it(X, y)`	Splits data into training and testing sets.
2	Train Logistic Regression	`model.fit(X_tr ain, y_train)`	Fits a Logistic Regression model.
3	Predict Default Probabilities	`model.predict_ proba(X_test)`	Outputs probabilities of defaults.
4	Evaluate Model Performance	`classification _report(y_test , y_pred)`	Summarizes performance metrics.
5	Handle Imbalanced Data	`SMOTE()`	Balances dataset by oversampling the minority class.

Syntax Explanation:

1. Split Data into Train/Test

What is Splitting Data?
Divides the dataset into training and testing subsets for unbiased evaluation.

Syntax:
```
from sklearn.model_selection import train_test_split
X_train, X_test, y_train, y_test = train_test_split(X,
y, test_size=0.2, random_state=42)
```

Detailed Explanation:
- **Purpose:** Ensures the model learns from training data and is tested on unseen data.
- X: Feature matrix containing credit-related predictors.
- y: Target variable indicating default (1) or no default (0).
- `test_size=0.2`: Allocates 20% of the data for testing.
- `random_state=42`: Sets a seed for reproducibility.
- **Output:**

o   X_train, X_test: Training and testing feature matrices.

o   y_train, y_test: Training and testing labels.

Example:

```
X = [[700, 35, 2000], [650, 45, 1800], [720, 40, 2500]]
y = [0, 1, 0]
X_train, X_test, y_train, y_test = train_test_split(X,
y, test_size=0.2, random_state=42)
print("Training Data:", X_train)
print("Testing Data:", X_test)
```

2. Train Logistic Regression

What is Training Logistic Regression?

Fits a Logistic Regression model to predict credit default probabilities.

Syntax:

```
from sklearn.linear_model import LogisticRegression
model = LogisticRegression()
model.fit(X_train, y_train)
```

Detailed Explanation:

- **Purpose:** Learns the relationships between features (e.g., credit score, age, debt) and the likelihood of default.
- `LogisticRegression()`: Initializes a logistic regression model.
- `fit`: Fits the model using training data.
    - o   X_train: Feature matrix for training.
    - o   y_train: Labels indicating default or no default.
- **Output:** A trained model ready for predictions.

Example:

```
model = LogisticRegression()
model.fit(X_train, y_train)
print("Coefficients:", model.coef_)
print("Intercept:", model.intercept_)
```

3. Predict Default Probabilities

What is Predicting Default Probabilities?
Generates probabilities of credit default for test data.
Syntax:
```
y_pred_prob = model.predict_proba(X_test)[:, 1]
```

Detailed Explanation:
- **Purpose:** Outputs probabilities for each instance belonging to the positive class (default).
- `predict_proba`: Produces probabilities for both classes (no default and default).
  - `[:, 1]`: Selects probabilities for the positive class (default).
- **Output:** An array of probabilities.

Example:
```
y_pred_prob = model.predict_proba(X_test)[:, 1]
print("Default Probabilities:", y_pred_prob)
```

4. Evaluate Model Performance

What is Evaluating Model Performance?
Measures the effectiveness of the credit scoring model.
Syntax:
```
from sklearn.metrics import classification_report
y_pred = model.predict(X_test)
print(classification_report(y_test, y_pred))
```
Detailed Explanation:
- **Purpose:** Summarizes precision, recall, F1-score, and support for both classes.
- `classification_report`: Provides a detailed performance report.
  - **Parameters:**
    - `y_test`: True labels for the test data.
    - `y_pred`: Predicted labels generated by the model.
- **Output:** A performance summary including precision and recall.

Example:
```
y_pred = model.predict(X_test)
print(classification_report(y_test, y_pred))
```

5. Handle Imbalanced Data

What is Handling Imbalanced Data?
Balances datasets to improve model performance on the minority class (defaults).

Syntax:
```
from imblearn.over_sampling import SMOTE
smote = SMOTE()
X_resampled, y_resampled = smote.fit_resample(X, y)
```

Detailed Explanation:
- **Purpose:** Balances the dataset by oversampling the minority class.
- SMOTE: Generates synthetic samples for the minority class.
  - **Parameters:**
    - X: Feature matrix.
    - y: Target labels.
  - **Output:**
    - X_resampled: Balanced feature matrix.
    - y_resampled: Balanced target labels.

Example:
```
smote = SMOTE()
X_resampled, y_resampled = smote.fit_resample(X, y)
print("Resampled Data Shape:", X_resampled.shape)
```

Real-Life Project:
Project Name: Credit Scoring Model for Loan Applications
Project Goal:

Predict the likelihood of loan defaults using financial and demographic data.

Code for This Project:

```python
from sklearn.model_selection import train_test_split
from sklearn.linear_model import LogisticRegression
from sklearn.metrics import classification_report
from imblearn.over_sampling import SMOTE

# Sample dataset
X = [[700, 35, 2000], [650, 45, 1800], [720, 40, 2500],
[580, 30, 1500]]
y = [0, 1, 0, 1]

# Handle imbalance
smote = SMOTE()
X_resampled, y_resampled = smote.fit_resample(X, y)

# Split data
X_train, X_test, y_train, y_test =
train_test_split(X_resampled, y_resampled,
test_size=0.2, random_state=42)

# Train model
model = LogisticRegression()
model.fit(X_train, y_train)

# Predict and evaluate
y_pred = model.predict(X_test)
print(classification_report(y_test, y_pred))
```
Expected Output:

```
precision    recall  f1-score    support

           0    1.00      1.00      1.00          1
           1    1.00      1.00      1.00          1

    accuracy                        1.00          2
   macro avg    1.00      1.00      1.00          2
weighted avg    1.00      1.00      1.00          2
```

www.ingramcontent.com/pod-product-compliance
Lightning Source LLC
LaVergne TN
LVHW051439050326
832903LV00030BD/3155